2020

TO SAVE AMERICA

2020

TO SAVE AMERICA

CHARLES A. PEARLMAN

gatekeeper press

Columbus, Ohio

2020 To Save America

Published by Gatekeeper Press
2167 Stringtown Rd, Suite 109
Columbus, OH 43123-2989
www.GatekeeperPress.com

Library of Congress Control Number: 2020944649

Hardcover ISBN: 9781662904134
Paperback ISBN: 9781662904141
eBook ISBN: 9781662904158

Preface

This book will explore all the presidential shortcomings and dive into his real legacy, the undoing of our national government in many different departments, especially his damaging federal court appointments. He is so full of hate, and so mean, he is unlike any other President. Completely unpatriotic and selfish, he doesn't read anything, doesn't even try to do the right thing and his callous stupidity is hurting our country; hurting people; and people are dying who shouldn't be dying. In short, he's an asshole (sorry, it's that he just so richly deserves the label).

There was so much bothering me about this administration, that I felt I needed to put it down on paper. If not, my head would just explode. Once I got started, I couldn't stop. I've tried to use many exact quotes and to fill the pages with my take on the significance of historical facts and important concepts that grip our lives, define our problems and our future. I also feel compelled to offer my solutions, throughout the book, to our biggest challenges from antibody testing to statue removal.

I hope my explanation of many of the medical subjects and other scientific innovations that are touching our lives today will be of use to you, and as interesting for you as it was for me in researching them.

Back in the 50's, we used to watch Captain Kangaroo on TV. Our favorite guy was a cartoon character named Tom Terrific, who put on his thinking cap, a funnel, to defeat Crabby Appleton, an evil inventor who was always trying to destroy the world. Like he would have an evil weather machine or some other evil invention; but Tom Terrific would outsmart him. Now, Crabby Appleton is our President. He needs to be defeated, so we have to put on our thinking caps.

Table of Contents

CHAPTER 1

The Shock

George Bush was an idiot (you know which one I mean). But this guy is so much more. He is resigned to be forever etched in the books as the leader of the racists and other right-wing fanatics, but he'll also be remembered for his lack of empathy, lack of regard for the truth, and his many psychiatric problems and childish defense mechanisms. He's going to leave behind a trail of destruction, caused by his rhetoric, his actions and his constant failure to act.

It all happened that Election Night in November 2016. That's when the National Nightmare began. I was all settled in to watch MSNBC and to relish the inevitable results that Obama, the first Black President, would be replaced by Hillary Clinton, the first woman President.

Rachel Maddow couldn't believe it; I never saw her speechless before. Steve Kornaki at the "Big Board" was just killing me as he tabulated county by county and struggled to predict each state. I'd been gleefully looking at the polls every day, and I wasn't waiting to find out who, but by how much, as the voters put the stamp on it and sealed the victory. Then Florida and North Carolina slipped away? All the polls agreed North Carolina was supposed to go for Hillary, but with that lost, it was almost OVER. A faint glimmer of hope - Nevada goes for Clinton. But then Michigan, Pennsylvania and Wisconsin made the lead insurmountable. And the Congress would be in Republican hands, at least for now

It was as if we were witnessing the Zombie Apocalypse. Where did they come from? From out of the woods and from whatever holes they crawled out of, they headed for the polls and scratched their X's on the ballots. From out of their trailers, they jumped in their pickup trucks they came by the millions to do their worst to our country.

Truthfully, I still have questions: How can a State be lost when you are 5 or 8 points ahead in the polls, consistently, every poll? Was there foul play here? No, it couldn't be, because no one was raising the alarm. Really. But there was supposed to be no path to victory. The polls proved there was no way to lose Florida, it was a lock!!

Nobody was more surprised than the President Elect, despite his insistence that he knew it all the time. Now, he would be able to declare that the American people were the jury that had just found him not guilty of every crime he (and his father) had ever committed. That was a conclusion that Sarah Huckabee Sanders, the highly unpleasant press secretary, would remind us of incessantly. We wouldn't be getting a look at those tax returns anytime soon, either. Even that dunce Pence couldn't believe it. He was resigned to defeat, now he'd have to play like he cared about the country, what a catastrophe for this lazy scarecrow.

I never imagined he would win, in fact I thought it was going to be the end of the Republican Party forever. He had managed to divide and destroy them irreparably. How could a party survive after it nominates a candidate who brags about a whole lifetime of assaulting women? Without being too graphic, let me just paraphrase that he was caught on video saying that when you're famous, women don't mind if you grab them by their private parts. "And when you're a star, they let you do it," he wisecracked. He later exonerated himself, claiming that it was just "locker-room banter." I had seen so many politicians resign over far less, I thought it was overkill, I almost felt sorry for him for the trouncing he was about to suffer. Although I did want to see him, and the rest of the Republican Party obliterated for eternity.

He had called the Mexican immigrants "rapists and murderers." Not even just some of them, but the way he said it, it was like all of them. He would build a two-thousand-mile-long wall. Oh sure.

He declared that federal district court judge Gonzalo Curiel, should recuse himself from a case in which he was involved, because of his Mexican ancestry. He accused the judge, who was born in Indiana, of not being able to remain impartial because he was "Mexican." His logic was that since he was a racist, and had clearly made racist statements, the judge wouldn't be able to conduct a fair trial. He was accused of civil fraud relating to his fake university. Who could vote for this guy? Was he seriously even a candidate?

He had insulted a Gold Star family, yes, he actually did that. And If you're not sure what that means, a "Gold Star" specifically refers to a family member who has lost a loved one in military service, usually while engaged in action. This is different from a "Blue Star" which refers to having a family member in active military service. The point is that our Armed Forces members are very much loved by their families and by all American citizens. I cannot personally even think of a Gold Star Mother without choking up. He compared their sacrifice to his own sacrifices, after all he had built many buildings. My jaw dropped; I was stunned. Nobody will vote for him now, I thought. Then this nationalistic WASP had called for "a total ban on Muslims" entering the country until "we" could figure out, "What the hell is going on." Well, I thought I knew what was going on. I thought there weren't enough ignorant racists to vote for this unbelievably hateful loudmouth. This is America. As a Jewish American, I found his intolerance intolerable. We are hands down the most detested minority, by all the bigots in the world. That's why we are hypersensitive to any assault against others.

He had called John McCain a "loser" and surmised that he was only considered a war hero because he was captured. "I like people who weren't captured," he told an Iowa crowd (and they still voted for him). I didn't like John McCain, voted against him, don't agree with his politics in any way, shape, or form, but he was a war hero. Ok, that did it. He's gonna lose so bad.

And there is something to be said for people who have served in the military and fought for their country before they want to send our kids into a war. Especially if they might be the type that would reflect on the realities and consequences they have experienced, before they give up trying to work things out peacefully. Too many politicians are willing to sacrifice others for the glory of the almighty dollar. Peace is always better all the way around. But maybe on the other hand, someone who never experienced the horrors of war might already be inclined to want to talk things out.

He had accused Obama of not meeting the constitutional requirement that a President must be a naturalized citizen, saying he had proof that Obama was born in Kenya, disqualifying him from being President and therefore "illegitimate". Ok, that was nothing but an un-American smear campaign. Campaign rhetoric gets a lot of license, but there was no factual basis for the claim.

He had been busted for making up two stories, for some inexplicable reason, about having many friends that perished in the World Trade Center on 911 and how he had seen "thousands and thousands" of cheering terrorists dancing on the rooftops in New Jersey across the Hudson River. Funny, nobody else saw those thousands and thousands of people. And nobody saw him at any funerals either. What a pitiful, sick guy. Didn't he have anything to offer? He was delusional, too.

Not only was he supposed to lose, but with the party destroyed, all that was going to be left was a bunch of racists, and gun nuts. Hopefully, I was just 4 years off: He has pushed the right-wing off into the Twilight Zone. But this nation is going to need a lot of repair, assuming they even can get rid of him this November. Never over-estimate the American electorate; they can let you down.

How could this be happening? I was so afraid, and I still worry, if we'll be shooting it out before it's over. I was worried that he could have his own Secret Police Force and have them wipe out our CIA or something far out and crazy or worse. After all, he had all that power.

Actually, I'm less afraid now. Now that I know what an incompetent idiot he is. But don't idiots start wars sometimes? Let's don't be complacent and just assume that we will wake up and it will all be over.

The Dancing Bear and his fool of a Vice President danced around and around at the Inaugural Ball, like they couldn't wait for it to be over. It was too boring for words. But the underlying fear was still there. Was this the end of the world?

"We won, get over it," said his fast-talking spin-master, Kellyanne Conway. Yes, we'll try. She represented his team and his supporters accurately. They were completely callous and enjoyed showing their contempt for most of the American people. Whether she knew it or not, she was letting everybody know that we were being divided into two distinct sides.

The Inauguration marked the moment when things began to crystalize. First, in an incredible display of cock and bull fiction, he was immediately claiming that his Electoral College victory was the biggest landslide in history. The President can't lie. Not a bold-faced lie. After a short while, we would learn that the defensive tactic that he would use over and over again to defend his horror-show actions would be to simply deny the truth. This has the effect of curtailing logical discussion because there is no premise from which we can begin to base our arguments. "I never said that," he would repeat falsely, so many times. Who cares if you can play a clip of him saying it, Fox News isn't going to play that clip because it doesn't fit the narrative. His ignorant base never sees the truth, so they don't even have a chance to judge for themselves. He lies without hesitation. He lies with indifference to the consequences.

It was impossible that this was happening. This was a mistake. I was still hoping against all odds that he could immediately be impeached, but it was a little spark that self-extinguished.

The Anti-Inaugural marches were planned in every city and village in the land. The huge total number of women and people who love and support women outnumbered his Inauguration crowd of raving lunatics 10-fold.

Then came the moment I actually thought could lead to a revolt. He went on and on about how his Inaugural crowd was the biggest ever. He couldn't stand the truth. Oh, the pain of it. More people had showed up for Obama's Inauguration, and his 'Press Secretary' Sean Spicer went on and on trying to repeatedly, unrelentingly deny what everyone could plainly see with their own eyes. There were official estimates from the Park Service, and comparative photographs clear as a bell. He's lying. I should be surprised. The President cannot lie. It was just so different from any President before him. Lying right to your face.

His supporters were repeating the lies. Fox News was repeating the lies. "Fake news" was their new battle cry. The truth was in question, we could no longer agree on the facts and argue about what they mean. This was the new reality. The Liar-in-Chief could gain traction against the truth by repeating his garbage over and over. Listening to him, I felt weak. Only my love of country could keep me going. My country was made up of honest, good citizens, who played by the rules.

Talking Politics with people took on a whole new twist. Even after hopping over these obstacles, if I finally could get someone to agree that what they saw with their own eyes was real, they would say, "Oh, well ok, he lies, but Hillary was worse", or "Ok, but I agree with the Republican position on this or that." The insane part is he's not losing any points for the fraud. It's OK for the leader of the Free World to lie? Are you kidding me, now?

Since then I think he's working on his 20,000th lie according to the newspapers and their fact-checkers who track these things.

When he gets in trouble, he'll use an outrageous lie, or do something blatantly unlawful or unconstitutional, or at least unpresidential to change the conversation. Generally, it gets him through to the next news cycle. It's pathetic how the Media can be manipulated and how the public's memory is so short. Overall though, that strategy is not working out so well for him, these days. But it has continued to be his *modus operandi*.

When he wants to put forth some outrageous conspiracy theory, or he just wants to smear somebody, he'll just preface it with, "A lot of people are saying some very bad things about _____" (fill in the blank) Then he'll say, "Not good!"

When he doesn't know something (which happens a lot), he'll say, "Nobody ever knew that."

When he ignores his intelligence reports and it comes back to bite him, he'll say, "Nobody could have known that." We saw this right away when President Obama warned him about Michael Flynn, the unregistered Turkish Foreign Agent, who famously led the crowd chanting, "Lock her up" at campaign rallies. Flynn sat in on the next meeting with the Russian Ambassador, anyway.

Bill Clinton, although not being perfect, was probably the best President in our history. He was a leader of all Americans. He could persuade anyone, as long as they were open-minded and intelligent. He was a Centrist, respectful of all sides. He inspired us to be good citizens and contributing members of a friendly society.

Hillary was the illustrious hero and champion of the Democratic Party. What an extraordinary candidate. She was the one who was actually qualified to run the government and she actually would have done so. I particularly love her for always having been the biggest supporter of the rights of disabled kids. She always fought for their right to be provided access to public schools in the least restrictive setting possible according to their individual situations and to be entitled to whatever resources they required. It's taken for granted now, but those kids used to be at the mercy of the often-unmerciful local school officials. They had no programs and didn't want to spend any money. A lot of kids were forced to stay at home.

She supports the Democratic platform, right down the line. She is smart. She wasn't the spy. It turns out the Accuser-in-Chief was the one in bed with Putin and who knows who else (which mobsters). She should have wheeled around and punched him in the nose during the debate, that time when he got in her personal space, lurking so closely behind her. She would have won and would have served us quite well.

Instead, we would endure years of lack of leadership that would cost us dearly and wreak havoc for decades to come.

CHAPTER 2

Then Came The Cabinet

First off, my favorite, the Secretary of Commerce would be Wilbur Ross, who was the former Vice-Chairman of the Board at the Bank of Cyprus, an island in the Eastern Mediterranean with offices in Romania, Ukraine, China and Russia. They were accused of money laundering and rumored to be the favorite of the Russian Mob. Why would he pick Wilbur to head up the Commerce Department? But it makes sense. With serious examples of ridiculous prices being charged in Florida and New York for properties, sometimes in excess of $100,000,000, combined with his refusal to show his tax returns, except basically over his dead body, it looks like we can figure out the Launderer-in-Chief's real profession. Why stop now? There's no shortage of dirty, dirty money out there. An experienced and powerful guy could clean it up so very, very easily.

Secretary of Housing and Urban Development Ben Carson is another real gem. He was the self-acclaimed Preeminent Pediatric Neurosurgeon from Johns Hopkins Hospital. What a joker. When candidate Carson was asked, as a physician, at the

Presidential Debates about childhood vaccines, instead of giving a scientific answer he advised, "some may be unnecessary," He remarked that the dosages needed to be spread out more (against settled medical practice), anything to try to get support from the anti-vax crowd. He is the worst doctor in history that I have ever heard of, and that I would NEVER take my child to in a million years. He has forsaken the medical profession for politics. He has aligned himself with the anti-science guy. He doesn't believe in Evolution. Sounds like the Scopes Monkey Trial didn't persuade him, maybe Clarence Darrow himself couldn't have convinced the Preeminent Doctor Carson.

Another physician at the Debate podium was that halfwit wannabe intellectual Rand Paul, who agreed with him. He wanted to be the cool guy with the anti-vaxers, too.

But the biggest blowhard, and eventual winner of the nomination and the election was the imbecile of the night when he immediately started crying that autism was becoming an epidemic. The anti-science people are partial to his brand of magical thinking, they voted for him. "I love the un-educated," he's been quoted as saying. Well, he loves their admiration and their votes.

Vaccines have been proven to be unrelated to Autism. Not by anecdotal observation but by actual scientifically designed studies. Also, Meta-analysis and systematic review of the current medical literature has conclusively dispelled the myths spread by these kooks and quacks. Although under the leadership that we are currently suffering through, ignorance was able to bring back measles with a vengeance to Brooklyn in 2019. Newsflash for all you anti-vaxers out there: Herd immunity only works as long as the immune population remains at high enough levels.

This depends on how contagious the infection is and how high the prevalence of the disease is. Herd immunity refers to a situation where a large percentage of the population is immune to a communicable disease. For instance, if 90% of a population has immunity, an infected person could only pass the disease to one out of ten people they come in contact with. Diseases like smallpox and polio have been made virtually extinct because of the heroic discovery of vaccines, and let's keep it that way.

Thank Goodness for common sense. The New York health officials started passing out $1,000 fines for refusal to take the measles, mumps and rubella (MMR) vaccine in the primarily Orthodox Jewish neighborhood of Williamsburg. The best story was of a group of Jews who sued to protest the fines, claiming the order was against their religious beliefs. The situation started to get hilarious when the judge turned out to be Jewish himself, and said he never heard of any such tradition, and threw the case out of court forthwith. When the Covid vaccine becomes available, a major health threat will remain: The World Health Organization refers to it as 'vaccine hesitancy'. Hopefully we will have a whole bunch of new leaders by then, to get us moving in the right direction.

Billionaire Betsy DeVos, the Secretary of Education, was best known as an advocate of tuition vouchers for private religious schools. She really doesn't need money herself, she is the sister of Blackwater founder, Erik Prince (you know, the company that sends all those independent contractors and security forces to Iraq). After marrying into the family fortune of the Amway pyramid scheme, it's safe to say money wouldn't be a big problem in her life. Ya think she might be a little out of touch with the average school kid and the average American family? While her husband spent his time lecturing his Anti-union baloney, and being buddy buddies with the Koch Brothers, she was content to fight for her religious values to be taught in the public schools. She is said to be trying to eventually end the right of all children to attend a public school in the United States, through manipulation of 'Charter School' systems. Another "perfect" appointment. I wonder if she's secretly happy that all the schools are shuttered right now due to Covid-19. Now she is making sure colleges don't give emergency coronavirus relief or grants to DACA students. Man, they hate those Dreamers.

Don't forget Exxon CEO, Rex Tillerson, Secretary of State. This random choice was actually suggested by Condoleezza Rice, but what the heck, he was rich enough. Applications to work for the State Department Foreign Service dropped by 50%. Finally, he called the boss a "Moron" before he was dismissed shortly thereafter. That's my boy.

I liked him better than Mike Pompeo, the pompous trampler of human rights everywhere (except if you are a recently conceived zygote, embryo or fetus) who reportedly has an eye on the White House in the near future. He likes to have watchdog Inspectors General fired, before they can dig up too much dirt on him. Then he has the nerve to outrageously claim that he was being investigated for the non sequitur accusation that someone was walking his dog to sell arms to his dry cleaners. This is typical obfuscation from this Administration. What dog was it? Was it the watchdog? Outrageous for sure. What a slap in the face to the American people to fire his own Inspector General. Nixon himself would be proud.

Let's talk about Mad Dog Mattis, appointed to head up Defense, without the statutorily required 7 years as a civilian.

He had 3 years, but big deal, anybody named Mad Dog would look good for sure. He didn't realize he was really working for Putin until we announced our premature withdrawal from Iraq in 2018. He resigned the next day. A few days after that, he was fired (you can't quit, YOU'RE FIRED – he so loves firing people).

Mattis has been relatively quiet as of late until the George Floyd debacle, chastising the President for his lack of leadership. He was one of many former Generals who criticized the militarized response to "noncombatant protesters" as making a mockery of the Constitution, stating the President was the" first president in my lifetime who does not try to unite the American people – does not even attempt to try. Instead, he tries to divide us." Good Dog.

Mark Esper has his job now, they used to call him Secretary Yessir, because he never uttered a word contrary to the President. Although never achieving much else besides establishing a reputation as a sycophant, he too, seems to have walked back the whole military response to Black Life Matters protesters. Where are you working next, I hope you have your next job all lined up, Mark?

His first Attorney General was Jefferson Beauregard Sessions III. Anybody from Alabama with a name like that had to be on the team, right? This schmuck came from Alabama with a banjo on his knee. A staunch Republican, he managed to cast every possible vote as Senator against women, minorities, gay rights, poor people, etc., every chance he could for 20 years. He was the quintessential pick. When questioned about his meeting with the Russian Ambassador Kyslyak, he couldn't remember this, and he didn't recall that. He could barely remember his own name. He basically stonewalled every question the Congress had, in defense of his client, the President. But unfortunately for the Colluder-in-Chief, he might have still had some tiny remnant left of his sense of duty. He recused himself from the Russia investigation. Or maybe he was completely in it up to his eyeballs. The President was openly furious, it was as if his own personal lawyer had dropped him. He sobbed to the NY Times, "…if he was going to recuse himself he should have told me before he took the job, and I would have picked someone else."

Couldn't he have just invoked attorney-client privilege? His exit strategy blueprints were already on the drawing board before the newspapers could print the morning edition.

He made a run at getting his old Senate seat back this November but got aced out of the primary by football coach and anti-mask Republican, Tommy Tuberville. Democrat Doug Jones will be sure to bring up the whole mess about Russia again anyway, but I'm sure he would have preferred to run against Sessions. If I squint real hard, I can envision Jones keeping his seat. I'm not lame enough to count on the voters in Alabama, but who knows.

His 5th Attorney General, William Barr is one of them there intellectual fascists. Appointed for vowing never to question the limits of the President's power, he reaches to the outer limits to justify his positions. He moved to drop the case against Michael Flynn, who already pled guilty (twice even) to lying to the FBI about the promises he made to the Russian Ambassador to remove sanctions that Obama imposed in response to Russian interference with our election. Serious stuff. Grasping at straws, Barr claimed the dirty cops had no basis for a counterintelligence investigation. That's one of those very sophisticated compilations of a pile of manure that we've become so used to hearing out of his twisted mouth. No AG has made a bigger farce of his office since John Ashcroft sang 'Let the Eagle Soar' after his endless abuse of the Patriot Act, instituted following the 911 attack. But Barr outdid himself recently when he was summoned to Congress to answer questions. He struggled to answer the question, if it was ever appropriate for the president to seek or receive foreign assistance in an election. He finally admitted that it wasn't appropriate. Then he proved he's the President's new 'fixer', and not the lawyer for the American people, and squirmed when asked about the firing of the U.S. Attorney for the Southern District of New York, Geoffrey Berman, who was investigating Giuliani and other White House operatives. He had lied when he announced that Berman was "stepping down". So, when he was grilled by Representative Joe Neguse about whether or not that was the truth, he answered, "He may not have known it, but he was stepping down. He was being removed". Then he laughed as if it was funny that he lied. He didn't care. C'mon people, it's time to impeach this United States Attorney General, William Barr.

Staying way down south in the land of cotton, the middle star of the Confederate battle flag represented Kentucky. And who better to represent a-way-down-there, than the wife of good ol' boy Moscow Mitch McConnell, the new Transportation Secretary Elaine Chao. If she learned nothing else at Harvard, at least she learned how to find the love of her life, Mitchie. LOL. I think she could have searched the world over and never found a man with a lower opinion of women.

She did such a great job as Labor Secretary under Bush, failing to insure federally required inspections in almost 15 percent of coal mines, which resulted in 47 deaths in 2006 before she finally got canned (not until the end of Bush's term) by the American people. Then it was time to go private for the next eight Democratic years and do more damage. But then the Republicans were back, and hubby hooked her up again. Nothing could stop her. Now teamed up with her husband doing the Congressional oversight, the unscrupulous wife threw him $78 million for Kentucky highway improvements, etc. What a chiseler she is, they make such a cute couple. Thanks a lot, Kentucky.

The do-nothing Cabinet fit right in with his agenda, which was no agenda. We'll be paying for this for a long time. A lot of good people are gone, a lot of good programs are gone.

CHAPTER **3**

Thanks a Lot

Was it the Evangelical Christians, racists, conspiracy theorists, Trailer Trash, Nazis, Fascists, male chauvinists, Xenophobes, plus the 2% of Businesspeople that would benefit, and the Republicans who were supposedly holding their noses? Was it the Anti-Treehuggers or Anti-Government fanatics bent on destroying our country? Russia definitely had a hand in it. Ticket splitters such as the Green Party definitely had a hand in it. With such a narrow victory, they're all to blame.

Let me tell you, that when a person claims to be an Independent, they're voting Republican. They just can't stomach the whole ridiculous Republican platform: Against the Environment, Women's Rights, Minority Rights, a decent living wage, Medicare for All, a sensible Immigration Policy, daycare for the kids and reduced college tuition, but willing to fight to the death for their right to own unregistered assault weapons. It's too big of a pill to swallow for many, even if they do think they're going to be saving a lot on their taxes when they get rich. Just like real Republicans.

I have trouble really focusing blame on the TV Star-in Chief. The people who voted him into office need to take the heat for this one. They need to take a hard look inside themselves. If you are one of those voters, next time just do the world a favor, don't vote. You haven't got the sense or the moral compass to make such an important decision. Don't trust yourself ever again. I don't.

JUST LOOK WHAT YOU'VE DONE:!!

You elected the Joker!

This month he got the heir to Goya Foods, Robert Unanue to praise him and pray for him while waiving cans of Goya beans around the White House and brag about how he's living the 'American Dream'. Was this a paid advertisement? He left an assortment of Goya products on the desk in the Oval Office with the big Eater-in Chief sitting behind it, smiling, reminiscent of The Price is Right. Which costs more, the Goya White Beans or the Goya Leche de Coco?

Nothing good is going on, that's for sure.

The Migrant Child Confiscation program was credited to have been dreamed up by favorite Senior Advisor Stephen Miller, who must have been influenced at an early age by the Pied Piper of Hamlin. Operation "Zero Tolerance" was immediately signed onto by the vicious Abductor-in-Chief as a way of discouraging immigration. When the public uproar from every corner was getting louder than the cheers from the xenophobic racists, AG Jeff Sessions went on radio to announce that if immigrants don't want to be separated from their children, they should not bring them with them. A lot of the children taken into custody were unaccompanied, 75% were over 15 years old. But many were toddlers, even infants separated from their screaming mothers and fathers and they too were later 'reclassified' as unaccompanied. The diabolical aspect of the whole ordeal was that there was no system of identifying which child belonged to whom, and the parents were being processed and shuffled around so much anyway, that all connections were just recklessly eliminated. The government simply abdicated responsibility, as the parents and children were scattered in every direction with no regard to them ever being reunited. It was one big nationwide game of Musical Chairs. We all remember the photos of kids in chain link fence cages, sitting on the cement floors with foil space blankets, sucking on frozen burritos. Six children have died since September 2018 following a 10-year period in which there had been no custodial deaths. According to the ACLU, many lawsuits have arisen due to all different types of child abuse while in government custody, and many more are anticipated. Sadly, the government has admitted that out of 2,500 detained children, there are still 120 who have not been reunited with their parents. Should we believe these numbers from people who didn't care enough to set up an adequate tracking system in the first place? Many activists and attorneys are propounding that the number is closer to 1000. Many could be reunited with their parents today, but it's not being done. Imagine if it was your child.

He will do it again, if he ever stopped at all. You can bet "Operation Zero Tolerance II" is in the works.

Stephen Miller is one of the only senior advisors left in the administration. Even after 80 members of Congress have demanded his resignation after his trove of emails with Breitbart revealed by Hatewatch showed him up for the white nationalist fascist that he is so deeply in heart. A Jewish neo-Nazi are you kidding? He never wastes time thinking about doing anything legally, when it's so easy to use executive orders to circumvent those bothersome laws that stand in the way. Oh! Let's declare a big national emergency, so we can steal money to build the wall. He's a real favorite of the Saudis and in particular the Prince of Abu Dhabi and Blackwater's Erik Prince (brother of Betsy DeVos). He makes sure we keep relations at an all time low with Iran and Qatar. He's been doing this since he was the stooge in charge of setting up back channels with every foreign country he could for the presidential candidate. He's still there in the White House laughing, too.

When warmonger John Bolton was named National Security Advisor in 2018, one thing that happened was they almost immediately disbanded the National Security Council Pandemic Unit. That has the appearance of being not a coincidence, like maybe Johnnie had a hand in it. It's another reason we were "blindsided" when the Covid-19 "came out of nowhere".

In March 2020, when the Governors were shutting down the states, the President started trying to do daily campaign rallies under the guise of daily briefings on the national response to the pandemic. He got up and spent hours every day trying to tell everyone they had plenty of Personal Protective Equipment when they didn't. Then he remembered that his commitment to never do anything at all about anything was setting his policy, which was no policy. It's really unclear whether he has ever invoked the Defense Production Act of 1950 in response to the shortages, but he did use it to order meat and egg producers to stay open (no mention of protection of the workers of course). But as far as equipment, he said he'd leave it up to the manufacturers to do it on their own. His team was bidding up the prices of supplies, driving up the cost for states to follow his advice to go out and get what they needed by themselves. Whatever his crew did come up with, they sold to middlemen to make sure they jacked the price up good and to further ensure that there would be no equitable distribution.

Then that little jerk Jarred somehow got ahold of the national stockpile of ventilators. With all the governors projecting shortages, especially in New York and Louisiana, the little punk said, "Those aren't the state's ventilators, they're ours." What was he going to do with them, sell them to Saudi Arabia?

It's so tiresome hearing the pathetic little pitch of "Federalism" all the time as an excuse for the federal government to do nothing. If anything, ever cried out for a national response, it's the current pandemic. Putting politics before governance on this issue was to exact a terrible price in terms of human lives and suffering. But every state is different, and unique goes the song, to which I answer in perfect harmony, that 50 knuckleheaded Governors would be lucky if they could put all their brains together to get somewhere in the neighborhood of a good plan. On their own, they don't stand a chance. We need a great plan, instead we have geniuses like the leaders we have in Texas, Georgia and Arizona. These guys have nothing to lose. Our neighbors can go ahead and suffer one funeral after another, and these dummies are only interested in maintaining their tax bases. And all those insurance companies, who give them all the campaign contributions, aren't losing a penny, either. The claims have never been lower, with everyone afraid to even leave their houses.

Wouldn't it have been the right thing to bring the whole world together and fight these problems together? Fighting together all the people of the world united against this scourge that will take 1,000,000 people before it's through. Oh no, not these guys. That would violate every principle of isolationism that Steve Bannon holds so dearly. He'd rather let them die, as long as his fortune survives.

These daily White House briefings were getting out of hand. His speeches were so chock-full of lies and inaccuracies, that he only succeeded in losing all credibility. Exactly what you would hope a leader wouldn't do. Dr Fauci was contradicting him 3 times a day. Then came the moment, after which the only thing left to do was to just pretend like the whole crisis had passed. It was almost funny. Disinfectant kills the virus? So, "maybe we can do something like that by injection inside, or almost a cleaning," he said, indicating his lungs with his hands? After turning himself into a laughingstock, the next day somebody told him to say he was just being sarcastic. His supporters needed some way out to explain why they support him when they're backed into a corner. "He was being sarcastic!" Like a talking point, something, anything. But so many people heard it and he wasn't being sarcastic. I like sarcasm. I know sarcasm. I'm sarcastic. The only time I'm not sarcastic is when I'm being facetious. He was being a big dope (with apologies to dopes everywhere). Just know that somewhere, a village is being deprived of an idiot. He's 1 pickle short of a barrel. He's such an idiot, he once told a judge that he wasn't going to make a U-turn, but the sign said NO U TURN. He's so dumb he sits on the TV and watches the sofa. He's so dumb he once stared at the orange juice bottle because it said concentrate.

I'm sorry, that was my little rant. I'll never do it again. It's just that sometimes I have to laugh to keep from crying.

It's the end of July and I am trying to reopen my offices, and we can't find disinfectant wipes, anywhere. And where are the N95 masks. More on this subject later.

What about that wonderful little group called Unite the Right? They united on April 12, 2017 to defend the statue of Robert E Lee, one of the devil incarnate leaders of the Confederacy 160 years ago. The Civil War was started by a conglomeration of tobacco and cotton plantation owners and brokers, who never had been able to compete against the rest of the world unless they were using slave labor. Their march turned into an anti-Semitic Nazi rally replete with chants of "Jews will not replace us," swastikas and the torches. Tons of people came out to counter protest and drown out the Fascists, and scuffles were breaking out. The site was the University of Virginia.

A young woman was tragically murdered when a car was driven into the crowd by one of the deranged marchers.

Where was our leader? He hustled down to his towers in Charlottesville, to stoke the flames of hate, as usual. Making sure not to say anything that would alienate his base, first he defended the whole purpose of the march, proclaiming that Lee was such a great "General". He raised arms against the United States and started the deadliest war in our history, and there have been plenty of them. And what was so great about that him? I would think he wouldn't admire a loser. Was it that sharp gray uniform? Was he a great military tactician? I suppose, but personally I preferred Francis Marion, the American hero of the Revolutionary War, who the British labeled as the Swamp Fox, who was renowned for his elusive tactics.

Then of course to keep the subject away from the murder, the Distracter-in-Chief dropped a big giant bomb when he said:

First, with the part about there being bad people on both sides, "I know it, and you know it," he bellowed.

But then, the memorable quotation for the history books, "you also had people that were very fine people, on both sides."

Really, so Nazi's are fine people. Or was he just parsing out the little fine part inside of them that admired Robert Lee. They wanted that statue to be preserved to remain as a symbol of their wicked past heritage, and the continued hatred in their hearts. Nothing fine about it. They also want to demonstrate their political power that keeps Confederate flags and symbols in places of honor, instead of in garbage heaps or Museums of Tolerance.

Like it or not, all Jews must stand tall amongst all Americans who remain constantly vigilant against any movement by racists and bigots of any kind. Anti-Semitism is a powder keg, that can explode without a moment's notice, and do a lot of damage if you're not keeping both eyes open at all times.

Let me tell the Racist-in-Chief that there are no fine Nazis. No fine KKK members. Even if under the hood, there's the police chief or the Judge, the bank president or the Mayor, they are the scum of the earth without any possible redeeming qualities whatsoever. But what about you? It's said that your father was a Klansman. In 1927 at the Queens County Memorial Day Parade he was arrested in Jamaica, Queens at a huge illegal Klan march for failure to disperse. The arrest record is all over the internet, no denying it. Was he just an onlooker, who failed to disperse, or was he Klan? The police report said all those arrested were "berobed". There are pictures out there, but who can tell with all those hoods. How about you? Did he dress you up in a little Kiddie Klan white sheet?

Those kids don't normally recover well, and this one for sure wouldn't.

Our nation would be better off without our lying President pretending how much really cares about history. We need to look at these monuments through the eyes of a people who were raped and murdered for hundreds of years. If Mississippi can change their state flag, we can start pulling down Confederate monuments right now. But what about Christopher Columbus, Andy Jackson, Thomas Jefferson, Geo Washington and the rest? Would you miss them? If they offend my brothers, I say who needs them? I never looked at the Father of our Country like that, but was he the Father of a lot of slaves? That's just not ok, these days. It's time to move out of the quagmire of hate that hurts us, today. It's time to break the chain, so we can break the chains.

Anyway, Mount Rushmore would look cool if they changed Washington and Jefferson to Bill Clinton and Barrack Obama. Is Roosevelt, ok? I don't even know. And I don't even care. I care about people's feelings before the 'historical value'.

The Washington Redskins have announced that will retire their name and logo effective immediately. The recent steady drumbeat against racism in America was forcing the hand of sponsors and the owners were obliged to give in. I know the MAGA President will moan about the nostalgic football days of old, and how football history should be preserved. He'll never let this one go unscathed. But this is so long overdue. And he has never raised a finger in support of our Native American brothers and sisters, so many of who suffer unimaginable lives in poverty, with lack of medical care and the some of the most underfunded educational systems in the free world.

Housing Discrimination was one of the little tricks he used to try to employ to increase his real estate empire. "Sorry, it's been rented," and then a White person would call about the same place. "Sure, come see it." Busted, no way out, he was forced to enter into a consent decree and to put an ad in the newspaper welcoming Black applicants to his housing units and inviting them to apply. He had to be forced to become familiar with the Fair Housing Act. His only excuse was that a lot of other landlords did it, too.

What's his excuse, now? Obama's 2015 Affirmatively Furthering Fair Housing rule halted funding for federal housing unless local governments 'affirmatively' protected affordable housing. In an overtly bigoted maneuver designed to get white votes in the "suburbs," he said, "There will be no more low-income housing forced into the suburbs." A deaf person could hear that dog whistle.

When Supreme Court Justice Antonin Scalia died in February 2016, I'm a little ashamed to admit it but I was really glad. Every word I had ever heard from him was antithetical to my own beliefs. As opposed to Jerry Brown, or Bill Clinton for instance with whom, for all intents and purposes, I always agreed with. Certain characters in politics are just that extreme. I was delighted that Obama would be getting one more appointment before he finished his term. I thought his previous picks of Justices Sotomayor and Kagan were just fine.

We all know how McConnell and the Republican Senators held up any all nominations and confirmations until after the elections. The first of two Supreme Court Judgeships was soon given to the new Appointer-in-Chief.

And he later gave Scalia a posthumous Medal of Freedom. Don't be too proud of yourself Antonin, he gave the same medal to Rush Limbaugh, too, so that award will be forever diminished. He probably gave the medal to that bigmouth for personal loyalty, conspiracy theorizing, and lying all the time. What an American!

As of now he's up to 2 Supreme Court Justices, 44 Circuit Court (Appellate) Judges and 112 District Court Judges. That's 2 out of 9; 44 out of 179; and 112 out of 673 total confirmed Justices. That's a lot. The Evangelical Christians have a lot of input but let's face it, a lot of these newbies are unqualified and a lot of them are really far out of the mainstream. We're in serious trouble and will be for some time.

Our only hope, however faint, is that it's a tough job; and they will have to follow precedence and that's a tall order, and they may not be bright enough to do as much damage as we fear. A little optimism never hurts. It needs to end; the Senate needs to tumble to the Democrats and we better pray Biden pulls it off. Replacing these judges is going to take a long time and the right leadership.

CHAPTER 4

Misogynist-In-Chief

It's hard to find a worse case of someone exhibiting more hatred and distain for women. The evidentiary set of words and actions that have shown him for person he is, is long and strong. What has he done for women, besides hold the carrot on the stick promising financial relief, that was never to come? He's never claimed to do any more than that. If he did claim anything, he'd lose support from all his woman haters. You never hear him advocate for women. Not to help with childbirth or mammography. Oh, no! Not to help with pre-natal care or birth control. Never! He might as well support Federal funding for abortions (Henry Hyde would have a heart attack: He'd come back to life and have a big giant coronary). No women's health issues were safe. In fact, he was perfectly happy to end Title X coverage for Planned Parenthood patients through some kind of dubious gag order. It was just more legal shenanigans. Millions of women were affected, and Planned Parenthood has been compelled to try to come up with private funding, always a daunting task.

They asked him in a 2016 interview about abortion. The nouveau-Republican (he registered as a Democrat in 2001, and not as a Republican until 2009) has views that coincide with whatever crowd he's hanging out with at the moment.

"Do you believe in punishment for abortion, yes or no as a principle," Chris Matthews asked him?

"The answer is that there has to be some form of punishment." First, he had tried to avoid answering, but he was really cornered and pressed hard and his weak, puny little mind couldn't figure out what to say.

"For the woman?" Chris probed.

"Yeah, there has to be some form."

In his 1990 interview in Playboy Magazine, he stated he didn't really have an opinion. "What the hell is yours," he snapped back at the interviewer. But that's consistent throughout all of his beliefs, he's sways whichever way the wind blows.

If he can call Nancy Pelosi a liberal, with a few disrespectful words thrown in for emphasis, and millions of voters pop up like grunions on the beach, he really likes that, so that's his new position. Basically, anything for a laugh. It's more entertainment than policy.

Childcare for working mothers – forget it. Education for women – forget it. Equal pay for women – ha!

When he bought the Miss Universe Pageant, he thought he would be so attractive to all the young teenage beauty queens. Maybe he thought he could rig the contest for the right price. What was he doing?

He talks about Jeffrey Epstein, the child molester, as being a friend for 15 years, "Terrific guy," he said. "He's a lot of fun to be with. It is even said that he likes beautiful women as much as I do, and many of them are on the younger side." Later, when Epstein was disgraced and busted, he changed his tune and said he had heard about him for 15 years, like everybody else, but he wasn't a fan of his and hadn't spoken with him in that time. There's a video of them laughing so hard together at some kind of party. Epstein didn't care about anything, he had been accused of countless cases of assaults by 13- and 14-year old girls, but it seems like he was way out of control. This maniac was finally stopped by the Public Corruption Unit of the Southern District of New York when they got him for sex trafficking out of his Caribbean mansion, and conspiracy. Another connection to teenage girls for the Monster-in-Chief.

Epstein's accused sex crime accomplice, Ghislaine Maxwell is currently being held without bail since the FBI popped her earlier this month. She's looking at a long, long, time away for setting up girls as young as fourteen years old with a lot of famous people. She's been charged with enticement of minors, sex trafficking and perjury, to be specific.

The thought might have even occurred to her that she might be able reduce her problems by turning states witness against a few of these lechers. Federal prosecutors are by all accounts interested in interviewing Prince Andrew, about his possible involvement with child abuse rings. Looks like maybe the Queen's son couldn't get enough girlfriends without help. Even though he was the Duke of York, let's face it, those princes just aren't that attractive, I never knew what Princess Diana saw in Prince Charles anyway, besides the obvious. This Maxwell probably has the goods on all of them. Maybe she could get a presidential pardon. This pig who berates women every day, couldn't find anything bad to say about his old friend Maxwell,

"I just wish her well, frankly," he told the press. He tries not to act like he's worried about her. Hopefully she doesn't end up hanged in her cell, like Epstein. Some still have doubts as to whether he may have been silenced rather than having committed suicide. I think he killed himself. I think he did it because he realized there was no way he could stop otherwise. Because he was a serial child molester. Maybe it's better that way.

I really would like to see the Pig-in-Chief be put away for similar assault crimes he has committed against women. The evidence is so overwhelming, and justice demands a conviction. Regardless of his claim that his election was a verdict of a jury, it's not the law. The popularity contest he won was conducted without any kind of legal procedural rules and is actually more akin to a lynching than a trial.

Many political minds have theorized, that while on one or more of his many romps to Russia, he may have done things over there that were documented, and that provide evidence of crimes not exactly subject to Statutes of Limitations. In other words – blackmail (They do that over there - They've been doing it for generations). What else explains how he cowers at Putin's every word. Journalists have posited that it may have been about sex crimes, or money laundering, or both. When you think about it, it does make a lot of sense. And no other world leader seems to wield that kind of power against him.

He's shown no regard for women. After having behaved so terribly throughout his lifetime, his own inferiority complex and self-loathing makes it impossible for him to ever respect women again. He can't even look a woman in the eye (not that they'd want him to). When he talks about the Governor of Michigan, Gretchen Whitmer, he refers to her as "that woman from Michigan". This kind of boorish behavior is not acceptable. I love women, I'll be on their side every time, and we won't tolerate animals like him! Wait till you see how he tries to deal with Biden's female running mate. It's going to be boys against girls again, like with Hillary, but this time the girls win!

I'm so proud of the way American woman revealed their power at the polls in 2018. Nancy Pelosi came right back. All the outspoken new voices in the Congress, punctuated by Alexandria Ocasio-Cortez. From a full-on sweep in Orange County, California, to a gay American Indian woman in Kansas, Black women, Muslim women, solid Republican districts flipped, like Iowa's 7th flipped by Abby Finkenauer, women voters and women candidates were getting it done. I was smiling from ear to ear. Even Alabama had something to say, they expelled that dirty Judge Roy Moore. Doug Jones was pretty good, by Alabama standards, but really? A Democratic Senator from Alabama? First one since 1990, before that they were the Dixiecrats. Well, Sessions had resigned his U.S. Senate seat when he was made Attorney General, so a special election was held in December 2017. Alabama Supreme Court Justice Roy Moore won the Republican nomination but then came the allegations of Leigh Corfman, that in 1979, she was just 14, and he was a 32-year-old district attorney who caught her at a very vulnerable time. While her mother went into the courtroom, she was told to wait outside. He pounced, he consoled her, he told her that she could give him her phone number, she could trust him, he was the district attorney, it was ok.

And, as my 'Me Too' sisters have been doing lately, a host of at least 7 other brave women came forward with horror stories of their own, that bolstered up the case.

It was too late to replace Moore, and for the Playboy-in-Chief, who had not supported Moore in the primary, he was now stuck with him. He had preferred the loser Republican Luther Strange, who was the sweetheart of the NRA and old simple-minded Karl Rove. But now it was Moore all the way, do or die. He hated to see a Senate seat go, and this guy was so guilty. He admitted to picking up girls (as an adult) at the local mall, but heck, he thought they were all at least 16, anyway. And this Ms. Corfman was very persuasive and convinced everyone. Former Republican presidential candidate Senator Mitt Romney said he believed her. Everybody believed her. Senator Lindsey Graham (R-SC) believed her.

But the President continued his "full-throated" endorsement, but he said it in a funny voice. He sort of droned, or moaned, "Vote for Judge...Roy...Moore." As if to say, he's scum, but do what you have to and be a good little Republican state." As it happens, I hadn't heard him use that funny voice again until the other day. Sick of dealing with the coronavirus, he said, at his famous Tulsa 'Big Flop' re-election kickoff rally, that he ordered his people to, "slow...the testing...down, please." He thinks he's funny when he uses dumb voices to say dumb stuff. It was so stupid, The White House had to scramble and say it was a joke, he was kidding. Peter Navarro even told the CNN cameras "C'mon, that was tongue-in-cheek". Nice try Pete, but then the President did what he always does and doubled down. "I don't kid", he continued. They don't know whether to cover-up for him, or whether he's going to stick both feet in his mouth as he's often prone to do. It's like watching the U.S. Open tennis matches, your neck gets so sore, turning this way and that.

This ridiculous babble, implying that more testing leads to more cases, of course followed right after he made unsubstantiated claims that we had the "most" tests, and the "best" tests. It must suck to be him. Trustworthiness is such an evasive quality. It's so hard to get people to trust you, and once you lose it, you pretty much have to document every single word you say after that. At this point, I wouldn't believe a word out of his mouth if he went and had his tongue notarized. He thought he would be the darling of his fan base, with a stupid remark like that, delivered with an extra special funny voice, but people are sick of the federal response to the pandemic, which is no response. It even fell flat with his hard-core supporters, who managed to fill almost one third of the 19,000 seat stadium. Flop Flop Flop.

74-year-old Herman Cain, former Republican presidential candidate died 40 days later after apparently contracting Covid-19 at that Tulsa rally, where he attended without wearing a mask. How many other less famous attendees are suffering the same fate.

Even our testing czar, Navy Admiral Pediatrician Brett Giroir says it's not due to more testing, because in addition to higher numbers of daily infections, we're also seeing substantially higher positivity rates. For instance, he noted that in Allegheny County (Pittsburgh Pa), 1000 people on June 17th showed 2% positive, 1000 people on June 29th showed 10% positive. No matter how you wrap that one up, it's a pretty stinky fish. Today they're talking about reports of a rate of 25% in Arizona testing positive. I would assume those aren't random tests but targeted at individuals with symptoms.

That funny voice could come with a whole psychiatric analysis, as well. Maybe it's not really him saying it. The man has issues. "Vote for Judge…Roy…Moore." Could he come right out and support a wicked child molester? No, but 'funny voice him' could come to the rescue. Well it didn't even budge the women of Alabama a little bit. The Republican men voted Republican, they're a special breed (or should I say inbreed). But it wasn't enough.

Jones squeaked out a victory by the thinnest of margins. Unfortunately, though, there were more than just a few disappointments and the Senate remained in Republican control. That's our country for you.

Will women voters make the difference again in 2020? Will women voters and Black voters unite (there's a thought that will make every Southern racist go nuts) and elect a Democratic Senator in Georgia, Kentucky, Colorado, Arizona, North Carolina and how about Iowa or Maine? Maybe even Alabama; that would be against all odds, but what if? A big rout is right around the corner.

Even Republican women need health care. They need reproductive health care, but they also need a medical system that accommodates all their health issues, and that of their children, even their husbands' healthcare affects them, too. Not only have 20 million Americans become newly covered since 2010, but 50 million Americans in jeopardy of being rejected for prior medical conditions have taken their place among the protected. The insurance companies must be losing it. They're stuck being the equivalent of a new single payer safety net. How can someone not buy insurance until they need it. I can't get earthquake coverage after the earthquake. Everybody loves coverage for pre-existing conditions, Democrats, Republicans, Independents (oh, who knows about them), Green Party, they all want it. If they agree on nothing else, they want that. What they really love is 'Medicare for All' but they can't admit it. Coverage for pre-existing conditions is pretty close, right on the edge, the insurance companies just need to be replaced by the government.

Try as they may, the Affordable Care Act programs are so popular, the Republicans can't get rid of them. Our idiot President claims he is doing more for women than anyone in history ever did by ending Obamacare, so they can afford to live their lives with all that money they'll save. All the wonderful things he's done to help women. Like leaving the pandemic crisis up to each individual state governor, killing hundreds of thousands, and shuttering businesses coast to coast. Like doing nothing about gender pay inequity. Like doing nothing to improve protection from spousal abuse, including showing no desire to confiscate firearms from abusive husbands, even after they've been convicted. He suggested that every teacher in every classroom should carry a gun. Maybe the rabbi should carry an oozie submachine gun, too.

He's done lots of other wonderful things for women and others. Like trying to cause a lot of grief for LGBTQ in the military, and just grief in general. Do you think he has any personal issues to discuss revolving around this subject? In psychiatry, a defense mechanism is observed to be utilized to allay an intolerable anxiety. Sometimes, people employ 'reaction formation', this is a very interesting neurotic mechanism wherein unconscious impulses that are unacceptable, are converted to the opposite behavior. A man, for instance, who envies women and would like to be a woman, needs to give speeches, railing against LGBTQ rights, in order to feel calm again. I'm just saying....

I predict that in my lifetime, we will have single payer insurance. The facts are that 35% of every healthcare dollar goes to insurance companies. In return for all that money, they give us a second opinion that nobody asked for. Not the doctor, and not the patient. It would be easy to make the metamorphosis, physicians are actually underpaid these days anyway. They, most of them, just want to help people and make a decent living. We'd save a fortune. Medicare for all. And you could always pay extra if you required a first-class private room, with sterling silver flatware and bone china. It would be perfectly ok for you to pay the difference yourself. Buy a supplemental policy to cover whatever you want. But basic equal care for everybody is pretty intuitive.

The pharmaceutical industry wants us to pay for all the research that will make them even richer. They don't spend anything, not a penny researching treatments that might benefit people, unless there's a payday at the end of the line. Preferably a pill, that you can take once a day, and that they have a monopoly on for 20 years. It's time to stand up for ourselves, and stop letting them charge whatever they think they can.

American Women are about to run him out of town on a rail.

CHAPTER 5

The Asterisk on the Record

The Impeachment by the House was on two counts: Abuse of power and obstruction of Congress. Although there was no Senate conviction, the stain is indelible. He's never been the same since, he's beaten. It's even taken a toll on him physically, let's say it's taken the jog out of his step, in fact, he can barely get down the stairs these days.

One thing was the withholding of $400 million in aid that Congress had mandated for Ukraine, whose borders had been breached by the Briber-in-Chief's handler, Putin. I kept getting confused because I always though then when a public official was accused of bribery, that they were the one getting the money; not withholding it as a bribe to someone else. But, no, this guy got that turned the other way around. Confusing, right? Anyway, Ukrainian Soldiers were getting killed waiting for arms because he needed some political dirt on Joe Biden. Plus, he would throw in a visit to the White House Oval Office! It was *quid pro quo,* this for that, an accusation to which the highly articulate chief of staff Mick Mulvaney remarked, "We do that all the time.... I have news for everybody: Get over it."

He wasn't about to get outdone by Kellyanne Conway. All those Republicans love saying, "Get over it." Every chance they get. It's like the playground at the junior high at recess. It's the new politics, the reality TV style politics.

The other thing was the Obstruction charge because of course Rudy Giuliani had to show what a fool he was in case anyone thought he had any understanding of the law whatsoever. Giuliani really got caught with his hand in the proverbial cookie jar this time. Since he was nothing, just a lawyer, he thought he wasn't breaking any laws. How did he ever become a lawyer anyway? He stuck his foot in his mouth every time he opened it. He would advise everyone to claim Executive Privilege. Those were the Presidents four favorite courtroom expressions:

1. "Hey! Executive Privilege, ya know?"
2. "Hey! Attorney-Client Privilege, ya know?"
3. "Hey! I refuse to answer on the grounds that I may tend to incriminate myself, ya know?"
4. Hey! I don't recall, ya know?"

Isn't it wonderful to have a gangster who knows his rights as the President.

There was a healthy sprinkling of witness intimidation: The tweets started to fly during the testimony of former Ukrainian ambassador Marie Yovanovitch, about her being removed and smeared for disapproving of Giuliani's mission to deliver the threats to the Ukrainian President and famous comedian, Volodymyr Zelensky. It was chilling and un-American, but the real obstruction was for hindering the House investigations, and withholding evidence from Robert Mueller. They even tried to have Mueller fired. The White House refused all subpoenas and requests for documents, and the President refused to testify, nor would he permit anyone else to do so.

Devin Nunes is a low I.Q. U.S Representative, who, I'm embarrassed to say comes from California. His persona bears further scrutiny. He stands for the Fresno-Visalia area, one of the few (7 out of 53) Republican districts in the state. In other words, he is a complete hick, as far out of touch with the rest of the state as imaginable. The former dairy farmer brings his big pile of manure with him to Washington DC and wherever he goes. He chastises environmentalists as being Marxists. He characterized California's decision to close schools in response to the coronavirus on March 31, 2020 as "way overkill." We'll have a "handle" on it "for sure by Easter," he prophesized. Oh no, he explained how he never told "healthy" people to "go out" to their local restaurant, "you can get in easy," he had counseled. He was merely encouraging going to drive-throughs. Ok so does that mean to "go out" to the "drive through?" So, "you can get in easy" to the "drive-through"? Wouldn't want to wait too long at the "drive-through." Even Sean Hannity, his number one clean-up guy, couldn't fix that one. Don't worry, those 100 and below IQ voters in Fresno still believe you.

Way back when he was Ranking Member of the House Intelligence Committee, he embarked on a mysterious journey bringing documents to the White House, that he had supposedly gotten from the White House about surveillance of the new President during the transition to the White House. So, he took the documents out of the White House to bring them back to the White House and the whole thing was blown up and shown to be a big stunt in cahoots with the President.

For the good of the nation, the House Intelligence Committee is supposed to be one of the least partisan committees in the Congress. How, therefore, would Devin Nunes ever even get on that committee in the first place? In fact, excuse me, who would pick Nunes for anything requiring any kind of intelligence.

Nunes has no shame. When he gets caught lying, he just slinks away, then comes running back later to the Koch Brothers billions for some more money. "NO COMMENT" should be carved on his tombstone for eternity.

He was involved in the Ukraine dirt scandal all the way. Rudy Giuliani and his criminally indicted associate Lev Parnas, together with Nunes were phoning each other, texting each other (thank you AT&T), trying to help get the Ukrainians to pretend like they were influencing the 2016 election as well as build some phony story against Biden's son's business. The fake scandal was obvious. But it needs to be clarified that the Ukrainian election interference baloney was being used to cook up a bigger stew full of interference, since the Russian scandal was becoming a big thorn in Putin's side. No, you're the interferer, no you are, back and forth it would go. This stuff works?

The other bad actors were who Bolton called "The Three Amigos". And I want to say that I loved that movie so much. Who was your favorite, Martin Short, Steve Martin or Chevy Chase? Couldn't he just have called them the "Three Little Pigs", or the "Three Blind Mice" or something else, oh, like maybe the three criminals?

There was the U.S. Ambassador to the European Union Gordon Sondland, we shall call him number 1. Fiona Hill, if you remember, testified that Sondland claimed to be operating in Ukraine under the President's authority. He testified at the House impeachment hearings wearing a $55,000 watch. The lovely Breguet marine chronograph in 18 karat white gold was emblematic of the way he donated his way into the coveted Ambassadorship. At first, he could not recall all kinds of key details, but then he got scared and was forced to admit, "I said that the resumption of the U.S. aid would likely not occur until Ukraine provided the public anticorruption statement we had been discussing for many weeks." In other words, until they dished up the phony scandal.

Number 2 was the bumbling Secretary of Energy, Rick Perry. To give you a short background, this crazed, bloodthirsty Texan signed more death warrants than anyone in history, 234, it's the world's record. I would almost pity him, having been born ignorant and all, but I'll save my tears for those he governed (those that didn't vote for him). Besides being the second worst Texas Governor ever (behind Bush), he was most famous for completely blowing himself out of the 2011 Presidential debate by not remembering his ridiculous idea to get rid of the three Cabinet Departments of Commerce, Education, "and the, um, what's the third one there? Let's see.... I can't. Sorry. Oops." I actually fell off the chair I laughed so hard. The EPA, Romney asked? And don't worry, Ron Paul consoled him by wanting to cut five agencies. The third one was Energy, by the way, the one that he heads now.

And bringing up the rear, Amigo number 3, Special Ukrainian envoy Kurt Volker. (not to be confused with Paul Volker, the Fed Chairman during the inflation until you go pop days of the 1980's). Those three knew their way around Ukraine from Kiev to Odessa.

Under the direction of Giuliani, the 3 (plus a few more) managed to put the Presidents political motives paramount to the security interests of the nation. Where shall we start, treason? Or, may I suggest extortion. There's always plain old misappropriation of Federal funds? That $400 million had been set aside by the Congress to help protect Ukraine, in order to make the United States stronger, safer and more secure. Now it was being dangled like a prize in a carnival.

Bolton described Giuliani as a "hand grenade, who is going to blow everybody up", and told Fiona Hill to let the White House know he "was not part of whatever drug deal Sondland and Mulvaney were cooking up." Where did he learn such talk? Maybe he might have had some experience with cooking drugs, or maybe dealing during his college days at Yale. It doesn't seem as if he was learning much law to be articulating that type of a description. Even if Bolton would have testified in the impeachment hearings, would it have made a difference to the Koch Brothers billions and their Senate lapdogs? Uh....no. Double asterisk: **He's still President**.

That second charge always bugged me. Obstruction seemed like a lot of technical legal violations, ok it's a serious crime, but it was kind of easy to get him to try to cheat, it was so easy it was almost like entrapment or maybe like shooting fish in a barrel. How could you miss. There were better things to pin on him.

For instance, the way he used the Russians to get elected, let's call it foreign interference in an election. That fits the textbook definition of an impeachable offense. Just because you solicit a crime on live TV in front of millions of viewers, you're still guilty. We can't sit still for his psychological 'flooding' and 'desensitization'. It's a crime, right before our eyes.

Another might be violations of the Emoluments Clause of the Constitution. For when he took money from Saudi Arabia for half his hotel rooms. This guy is under the impression that one of the big benefits to becoming President is that you get to abuse your authority for your own personal gain. To increase his fortune, he has vacationed at his own hotels and golf courses worldwide more than 300 times. Wait a minute. 365 days per year times four years is 1460 days, when you divide that by 300 vacations that's less than a vacation every 5 days. The most nauseating part of that little equation is that he's President for 1460 days, by the way. Each time he's accompanied by his entourage. We're talking about Secret Service agents, other security, VIP guests (?), assistants, other employees, and plenty of sycophants all treated on the US credit card to an all-expense paid extravagant holiday. And the bill gets paid directly to him. He's rescued several of his failing properties from bankruptcy in this fashion. He just charges himself as much as he wants. Who cares? He seems to answer to no one, so he continues to keep stuffing his pockets. A three-day 2018 trip to the UK was said to cost $25 million in security alone, plus the associated costs of over an estimated one thousand people chaperoning him. I hope he got to stop over in Scotland or Ireland to visit some of his golf courses.

You know what, if I were the President I'd stay home and watch a movie and use all those public funds to feed starving children or something.

One of my favorite impeachable offenses he has committed will be exposed when we finally get his tax returns. It's my guess that we will easily find enough evidence of money laundering to bust him permanently for this highly serious offense against the

United States of America. Let's get him for that. That's what he really is and has been for a long time. While we're at it, let's get a look at his overall financial picture and see what other things he can't explain. And don't forget tax evasion, when we find that. He's that, too.

He also committed the heinous act of forcing all those immigrant children out of their parents' arms under false pretenses, an act which has been branded as "torture" by the United Nations Human Rights Council.

I think it would be ok at this point to wait until he's voted out and try to bring him to trial and let him serve some time. Just like the rest of us would have to if we tried any of this.

The problem is it would be nice to have fair elections again. One reason the House pushed through the Presidential impeachment was to dole out punishment for seeking foreign interference in our elections. He came right back after the Senate acquittal, and propositioned China for help. The House had bipartisan support for election security legislation, but McConnell wouldn't have any of it. That earned him the nickname "Moscow Mitch". It is said he actually hated that. Not like Brer Rabbit saying, "Whatever you do, don't throw me into the Briar Patch." It truly brothers him. Good, he bothers me. He definitely deserved the name. He's a crooked, win at all costs, pawn for his financial supporters. A typical Republican politician, a real shyster. I would challenge that he believes not a single word of what he says. For him it's all about the business. Hopefully a miracle will put him into retirement. He's done enough damage. Another doubtful Democratic senate seat takeover. Go Lieutenant Colonel Amy, I saw one poll where she was ahead +1. She put her challenger, Booker away, let's keep our fingers crossed. With what we've all learned about the Senate lately, who the heck would care if Moscow Mitch won reelection anyway, as long as the Democrats took over control of the Senate? The minority party Senators are like a bunch of chattering mouthpieces anyway. Who listens to Senator Chuck Schumer now? If he becomes Majority Leader, everybody. Especially with a President Biden and an expanded Democratic House Majority. The whole wide world will be listening.

There are going to be a lot of problems on election day. Until the Supreme Court threw out key voting right protections in 2013, the burden of proof in certain states, was on the government to prove that any regulations they sought were not discriminatory. This was because primarily in Alaska, Arizona, Texas, Louisiana, Alabama, Mississippi, Georgia, South Carolina, and Virginia, and certain counties mainly in North Carolina, Florida and even California, it was thought that any voter restrictions had, for so long, been targeted at restricting Black voters. When the Supreme Court ruled that these practices were no longer indicative of the current conditions, everyone knew the doors would be open to every state to knock us back to 1965. It was obvious and easily predictable. After all, so much money had been dumped into state legislative races, the Republicans were already running roughshod in a lot of statehouses. Nowadays, the voters have to put the gloves on and defend their right to vote. And don't think we won't.

Georgia Governor Brian Kemp will do anything in his power and then some to keep his state's electoral votes from going Blue. Look what he did to cheat Stacey Abrams out of being Governor. He was Georgia's Republican Secretary of State, so he essentially presided over his own election. He certified the outcome of the contest that was rife with fraud, declaring himself the winner. A little trick called "exact match" voter registration regulations required that voter applications be identical to state or federal records. The purging of thousands of eligible qualified voters coupled with a lack of functioning voting machines in some select precincts was enough to flip the election to Kemp by less than 1.5%. In one county, a large cache of absentee ballots was not counted, requiring a federal judge to step in and order their preservation. One group of voters that were cheated were the 53,000 Georgia voters who had a hyphen in their names, who were predominantly Hispanic or of other minority groups. Plus 87,000 casualties of Kemp's strict late registration regulations would alone make up for his margin of victory. There are so many other examples of his unethical violations of the public trust. One crime after another. After all, it was his full-time job to deny the right to vote to minorities and other Democrats. This is the type of person our world is facing, and we cannot back down to the job of seeing that he makes an early departure. So far, he was amazed to learn that Covid-19 could be transmitted by asymptomatic carriers: A real "gamechanger," he said, he was one of the first to open his state up for business, with disastrous consequences. Haircut, anyone?

The obvious conflict of interest in the shameful gubernatorial race was really only par for the course in Georgia politics, but the experience has inspired intense national debate around voter suppression. Millions of Democrats are on guard against any hint of election fraud, now that the Republicans have tasted the sweet fruits of this chicanery once again. Under the pretense of voter fraud, registered citizens are often kicked off the rolls for partisan gains. Two million Georgia voters in 2011 were required to present Social Security records to verify their eligibility. In 2019, 234,000 Wisconsin voters were targeted in Madison and Milwaukee. That rotten, lying, union busting Scott Walker just loved disenfranchising students and minority voters, who had to scramble to re-register, but some never even knew about it, or thought it wasn't worth the trouble because it would be too difficult. Maybe they were a little busy with school or work. Many would have been first time voters.

This country has a long history ever since the Jim Crow laws instituting poll taxes to inhibit Blacks and poor white voters. To this day Georgia still requires absentee voters to pay the postage on their mail-in ballots. They just can't let go.

Beware of legislation like the famous Texas voter ID law requiring identification to vote, that was struck down as discriminatory. In 1986, Coretta Scott King's voice was heard in clear protest. The great Rev. Martin Luther King worked tirelessly to raise Black people up. He could have been paraphrasing Moses himself, in 1965 when he said, "Let my people vote." It seems like ancient history. The 'King' of nonviolence spoke often in Los Angeles during the war in Vietnam, where so many young Black men were serving and dying. I saw him speak there and marched with him down Wilshire Blvd. So many thousands of Black soldiers who went to Vietnam were from Texas. They paid for the right to vote with their blood. That has been the price America has paid for centuries. Texas is now so proud of closing over 500 polling places in overwhelmingly predominantly minority communities. They want to make it harder for Black people to vote. How sickening and disgusting. And don't you know, those Republican redneck Texans love to wrap themselves in the flag as they trample on people's rights.

What a travesty. Have they no shame? That's why Malcolm X, who was never accused of being nonviolent, delivered his famous 1964 speech, "The Ballot or the Bullet".

Beware of people like the Koch Brothers in 2011, who got caught when they funded a huge effort to mail out false mail-in ballot deadline information to Democrats and snickered while claiming it was a typographical error. Why would they spend their precious money to send out accurate, helpful information to Democrats? I rest my case, guilty as charged.

Beware of voter intimidation like in 2018, when a bus full of senior Black voters in Louisville, Georgia (where else?) were made to get off the bus on their way to early voting. The Republican sheriff declared it a violation of some county ordinance. What about the constitution?

There are so many examples of voter suppression, so many cases in our nations checkered past, they could fill an entire book; no entire volumes.

The big test is coming up in November. You know this loser is pulling out all the stops (he'll literally stop at nothing). The best offense is a good defense: He's saying that mail-in ballots are an easy target for fraud. Of course, that's never been shown to be the case. In fact, I don't think I'd ever even heard of that before. Why would his opponents need to cheat, they're leading in every nationwide poll, and in almost every "battleground" state? Oh, those are the fake polls, combined with the rigged mail-in ballots. Even his nut case supporters will find that combination a little far-fetched. How will he prove that absentee ballots are prone to be susceptible to fraud? Simple, like he always does: By repeating it over and over. He's already said it dozens of times, about another hundred times and his base should be on board.

His new Postmaster General, appointed in May 2020, is Louis DeJoy, a big donor and fundraiser. This hack is trying to destroy our US Postal Service right now, to make it as hard as possible for mail in ballots to be collected. Ok Louis, 18 U.S. Code § 1703 covers Delay or Destruction of Mail. You better read it carefully Louis, it provides for up to five years federal prison time. I'm sure a few more additional appropriate charges can be combined to put you away for the rest of your miserable life. Don't depend on a pardon, Louis, your partner in crime might be out of office by then.

In effect the Thief-in-Chief is trying to steal the election by forcing everyone to congregate at the polls in the midst of a killer pandemic if they want to vote. Risk the virus to cast my ballot? Not a problem, I wouldn't think twice about it. I'm not kidding. I'm voting at my local precinct on Election Day. I'll be dressed like an astronaut. I don't play. When I was a kid I got kicked out of recess. Do you know why? Because I don't play.

He expects every Republican Secretary of State to line up for him and put in the fix in every way they can, so he can have the slightest chance of coming out on top. The scary part is, most of them will if they can. These are political stooges who serve at the pleasure of their campaign contributors, and political action committees. They are formidable foes, but they can be beaten if the people flood the polls and make their voices heard. The ghost of Representative John Lewis will be standing guard. He shed his blood on the bridge in Selma back in 1965 for Black people to have the right to vote. We need to be determined, stay positive, and just to be safe, put our lawyers in all the polls and courthouses, ready for action.

Don't worry about him accepting the results of the election. It's not up to him. It's not up to the military. It's up to the voters, and he can't stop the people. He's already a lame duck President with Biden leading by 15 points in the latest ABC-Washington Post poll. He'll do his worst after his defeat, until January 20, 2021, but then he's out! His term will be finished. And the whole time we'll be left to shake our heads and keep asking how he won in 2016, so we can stop history from ever repeating itself.

CHAPTER 6

Breitbart – Bannon – The Mission

This President never loses sight of his own best interests. He quickly realized that had been entrusted with a lot of leverage over the Federal Court System. He now could control the United States District Court for the Southern District of New York, both by judicial appointments and authority over the prosecutors for this very unique jurisdiction. This district hears cases concerning the stock market on Wall Street and other major financial institutions, and even more interestingly, the President's own businesses as they lock horns with federal law. One day he will no doubt gloat to the American public, "You were stupid enough to give me the power." As when be confessed to tax evasion, saying, "That makes me smart."

Never before had an American President announced his serious intention to run for a second term at his inauguration. He needs the power of the presidency to compete in business, he has never shied away from unfair competition and unfair practices. All he had to do was to stay cool with Putin, nobody would blow his cover, and he'd be able to continue his unlawful business totally unchecked in the USA. What an abuse of his trust. What a violation of his Oath of Office. What treacherous and greedy exploits is he getting away with? And at the same time his total abdication of his pledge to protect and defend the country reveals him as a traitor. He loves money and power. The longer he stays in power, the longer he become richer and more powerful.

But it appears his chickens are coming home to roost: The NY Times, Wall Street Journal, and NBC are all confirming that Russian spies paid cash bounties to the Taliban for killing American troops and their allies, during Afghan peace talks. Six U.S. servicemembers were killed there as of February this year. Hundreds of pro-Afghan troops are still dying every month, not to mention countless civilians. The President was briefed in March 2020, did nothing, and in June, when he met with Putin, he came out of the meeting determined to put Russia back in G7, and to pull troops out of Germany. Nobody can manipulate him like Putin. But maybe Putin pushed too hard this time. Families of our fallen heroes are going to want answers. They are going to want an explanation for the total abdication of his oath to "provide for the common defense." This little trick may linger and show its ugly head every so often.

Barbie doll White House Press Secretary Kayleigh McEnany can flash her twisted sardonic smile and claim that he never was briefed on the Russian act of war, but that's even worse. In March, the White House's National Security Council had a big meeting, now they are claiming he didn't know because he doesn't read his intelligence briefings. She said, he "does read" the PDB (President's Daily Briefing). He "sometime consumes information verbally." She went on with more bull, "This President, I'll tell you, is the most informed person on planet earth when it comes to the threats we face." So, he didn't listen when they told him verbally? That's not an excuse. Sorry, like a lot of Americans, I get super raging furious when it comes to our soldiers getting killed. Any other President would have imposed severe sanctions. This one imposed favors. There is a particularly repugnant photo of him shaking Putin's hand in June.

Now he's saying it isn't a credible report. So first he was never briefed, then he was briefed, but not verbally, but he didn't read it, but then there was information missing. But now Barbie is saying, "You've got to be kidding." He knows more about this than anyone in the world.

Or a fourth possibility is that he is such a nut case that they gave up trying to brief him because he flies into a rage whenever U.S. intelligence has warned him about Russia.

Pick one, it doesn't matter. He still to this day has taken no action to stick up for our armed forces. Even if he took covert action, he should publicly state that we won't sit still and be attacked like that. He only states that it's not true. He does not claim that the intelligence agencies have advised him that it's possible that it's not true, though.

The thing that is true is that this is just another true story of dereliction plus treason that reaches beyond the horizons of our understanding. It's true because nobody could make it up because no one would believe it.

When he first started his run at the presidency, when he thought it was a joke and couldn't possibly succeed, he hooked up with Steve Bannon. Campaign manager Bannon introduced him to a base of anarchists and/or Americans that had become 'the disillusioned'. These losers were a way bigger group than was realized. People who couldn't make it in one way or another and had given up on the American dream. They wanted vengeance; they found solace in the new dream of destroying the system they couldn't fit into. Bannon and the rest of the creeps over at Robert Mercer's firm Cambridge Analytica, were instrumental in helping with strategies for raising money for organizations like Leave.EU. The only thing that remains to be proven is any illegal foreign fundraising in a British election. Sort of like the foreign involvement in our election by Russia. When Bannon took over Breitbart News, he cooked up an alt-right combination of American and European right-wing extremist groups. Their philosophy emerged with florid hostility toward traditional Republicans, who were accused of allowing capitalism to be eroded by liberal-style compassion. All his distorted tales of the collapse of Wall Street in 2008, and middle-class socio-economic problems throughout the country usually just boiled down to the growth and unsustainability of the welfare state. How boring.

So many people are mystified about exactly what these guys are trying to do. Under the pretext of eliminating all traces of the Obama legacy, this new political order is plunging forward on a path to destroying our government. They have a fundamental principal of getting the Federal Government out of everything. In this way, nationalism and capitalism can proliferate with impunity. Without all those pesky regulations, the biggest and most powerful could steam roller over everyone else on their way to invincibility. No wonder the Koch Brothers ($50 billion) and Sheldon Adelson ($30 billion) were eager to jump on board. They needed more money to force their sick social agendas down our throats. For sure they can't abide by separation of church and state. They can't tolerate women's rights. They want to Make America Great Again, meaning they want to go back to the days of slavery, when they believe the Black people were happy to live a carefree life on the Plantation. They're serious. The scary part is they have a plan to get there! They want to start by methodically eliminating education, medical care, food, clothes, shelter, and eventually you'll be so broke, you won't be able to own anything. You don't own the property; you ARE the property.

From the Federal Housing Administration to the Affordable Care Act they want to get rid of it all. From the Environmental Protection Agency to the public-school system, it all offends them terribly. Every man for himself. Let's not work together. Obama is more or less just a code word. His name is a convenient label to pin on a program, to avoid having to discuss the merits of whatever target they're aiming at destroying. "The disaster known as ObamaCare," need he say more?

One office after the other, one regulation after the other, one protection after the other, disappearing overnight while you sleep. I wish my wrinkles would disappear as quickly.

The big myth is that the liberals don't believe in capitalism. Don't you know Biden also wants to open up the borders completely wide open all the way so we can provide free medical care to the whole world? That's a MAGA copywrited salespoint right there.

I need to argue that capitalism needs to be practiced within a system of laws. If you allow companies to dump toxic waste into the river, so they get rid of it for free, and they profit, becoming big giant monsters, the people downstream are going to be injured. If you allow an industry to manipulate market share through dumping of products at prices below cost, fair competition will suffer afterwards. If you allow companies to illegally bust unions to keep labor costs down, workers and their families aren't going to be able to live decent lives. Capitalism should reward the brightest and most industrious, not the criminals and cheaters.

Bannon was ready to fight. He understood the Electoral College system. California, New York and Illinois are solid Blue states. But this is a Federal system, where each state gets "Extra Credit" just for being a state.

Your vote counts almost 3 times more if you live in Montana, Alaska, Delaware, South Dakota or Wyoming. They each have only 1 United States Representative but all states have 2 Senators. So, they get a total of 3 Electoral Votes each.

I vote in California, the state with the most Electors. My vote couldn't be any weaker.

California's 55 Electoral votes include but 2 votes for our 2 Senators. Our 2 Senators are lost in that crowd. Similarly, so many other 'Breadbasket States' with 4, 5, 6, or even 9 or 10 Electors pack a powerful punch in the Electoral College for representing such a relatively small number of voters. So much for 1 person 1 vote.

But between the highbrow Bannon and the Cheater-in-Chief, they had a whole deck of Aces up their sleeves. They were easily converting the under-educated under-employed suckers into racist xenophobes. "Build the Wall. Who's gonna pay for it? Mexico!" they chanted. There's one born every minute.

In 2019 he was still saying, "Build the wall," but this time in Colorado. I am telling you he actually said that, he said it in a speech in Colorado. But just for clarity, he was talking about putting an actual wall like on the Colorado state border. His Colorado fan base jumped up and gave him a standing ovation. Later he said he was kidding. Maybe he knows something I don't know. I thought, if nothing else, I have a fairly good sense of humor. But I don't get the joke. The only thing funny about it is that he was serious, meaning he doesn't know where Colorado is on the map in relation to Mexico. Didn't he see the Colorado license plates with the Rocky Mountains on them? He probably thought those were the Sierra Madres. Now with the virus rocketing out of control in Arizona, Mexico wants to shut down the border in Nogales to Americans. Maybe they're finally going to pay for the wall. That's priceless.

Another beauty was that Hillary was a traitor who was sending some kind of surreptitious emails from a server in the basement. "Lock Her Up," was their rap. Scott Baio, Michael Flynn, the mental midget Ted Nugent, not to mention the fake wrestler and fake former presidential candidate Hulk Hogan, a true politician in his own right, all joined the chorus.

In 2017, some postings began under the name of Q. Hillary Clinton's arrest was imminent, they claimed. Satan-worshipping pedophiles rule the world, don't you know? This may have been an individual or a group dedicated to fake conspiracy theories. Another big whopper was about how the deep state was involved in a secret mission against the President and his base. QAnon demonized Hollywood, Democrats, especially George Soros and Hillary Clinton as child-eating cannibals. Their followers love to rail against secret cabals within the government and inexplicably seem to be easily convinced that the most outrageous stories are somehow the stone-cold truth.

The Rothschild family is a satanic cult. Various anti-Semitic, racist and plain conspiracy rants have recently led Twitter to disable about 7,000 Q accounts. This is a necessary step to prevent coordinated brigading of tweets against individuals and groups that can be very devastating to the victims. At least five current California Republican candidates for U.S. House of Representatives are regularly citing QAnon garbage, and that's just in California. QAnon is currently involved in the resurgence of the Pizzagate fable about a restaurant which was really a front for a human trafficking and child sex ring. Pizzagate was unequivocally debunked in 2016 when a man with an assault rifle, trying to rescue the children, shot up the restaurant, no one was hit, and he was sentenced to 4 years after apologizing in court to being "foolish and reckless." Bannon should make the same apology, but I think 4 years would be a little light of a sentence for him.

In a blatant abuse of presidential power, our sly President just commuted the sentence of the 'Dirty Trickster' Roger Stone, who was convicted of 7 counts including witness tampering. "You are a rat...Prepare to die" he told Mueller's witness, Randy Credico. Then Stone threatened that he would "take that dog away from you" in reference to the witness's pet. He does sort of resemble the wicked witch in The Wizard of Oz ("I'll get you, my pretty, and your little dog, too"). Among the other six counts he confessed to were lying to investigators and lying to Congress. Stone was protecting the President when he lied about communications he had with White House officials when questioned during the Mueller investigation. Days before his 40-month prison sentence was to start, he gets a pass.

In April 2020, a trove of emails from 2016 between Stone, Julian Assange, and the Russians revealed Stone's involvement in hundreds of fake Facebook accounts, blogs and conspiracy theories.

People are saying he was threatening to sing about everything he knew, or he was being rewarded for obstructing justice during the investigation. Maybe as re-election hopes are fading, the Loser-in-Chief is just looking for some more dirty tricks. You know he's going to need to pull a rabbit out of his hat, and nobody is more conniving than Roger Stone. This crafty old man with the odd-looking hat has a lifetime of experience of total disregard for morality, legality, and the harm he causes to others. Stone, a frequent contributor to Breitbart News, brags about his personal style: "Attack, Attack, Attack – never defend. Admit nothing, deny everything, launch counterattack."

Let's remember that upstanding citizen and media mogul, David Pecker, he would be such a great asset to the campaign. The chief at American Media Inc. was the owner of the National Enquirer at the time, when he was caught on tape talking about the best way to pay off Karen McDougal, the Playboy bunny who claimed to be the girlfriend of the Republican candidate himself. There was plenty of hush money between Pecker and the Stud-in-Chief's lawyer/fixer Michael Cohen. Unfortunately, it violated all campaign laws in all directions. First, Michael Cohen was spending hush funds that were from the campaign coffers; that's illegal. Next, a tabloid empire paying hush money for you isn't just seedy, it's also an undeclared campaign donation; another violation of the law. Oops, David Pecker in legal trouble again. Good thing he has about hundred attorneys.

The Enquirer was famous for employing the 'catch and kill' technique. That's when they buy the rights to your story, and you think they're going to make it public and the world will finally know the truth. Then the joke's on you when they kill it, and it's Hush, Hush Sweet Charlotte. They own it, you can't tell it to anyone else. You sold it to them.

He had some more ideas to help his buddy get elected. He would spread wild pseudo-rumors ('pseudo-', because not many people actually believe them) about Hillary Clinton, because it couldn't hurt, and anyway at the very minimum it would help to distract the public from any real issues that were affecting the United States. Hillary had an alien baby, no, not from another country, from another planet. She had six months to live, two strokes, lung cancer, and a nervous breakdown. His next project was to try to smear Harvey Weinstein's accusers. Although he was thoroughly and plainly unsuccessful in keeping old Harv out of the slammer, at least he gave it the old fraternity brother college try. These good old boys really stick together, they're as thick as thieves.

But the special campaign trick, the clincher that put the candidate over the top was the Russian's involvement. Along with WikiLeaks and Julian Assange, the Democratic National Committee server was hacked, and President Obama was hesitant to blow it open, because he didn't want to weigh in heavy, and be accused of influencing the election. Besides, Clinton was so far ahead she would win anyway (at least I wasn't the only one who thought so). Putin marshalled all the resources of the best computer minds they had to create Facebook algorithms teeming with fake stories and every social media trick the internet had ever known. They used all kinds of human-interest stories to drive traffic to propaganda and misinformation. Cute kittens playing. Auto-dialers, foreign phonebanks, millions of dollars in computer analysis, Putin delivered the winning edge for his old friend and chump. With all the deals he's done with Russian, it was obvious that he was under their thumb.

The Russian expression, kompromat, describes a situation where damaging evidence is collected which can be used to create political or legal problems for someone who has been compromised. The Russians have long been famous for sexpionage. But they are equally skilled in financial games with embarrassing outcomes. It's like Russianopoly, and you go directly to jail. How badly he's stuck, who knows? But we have a lot to lose with Putin having such a close ally in the White House.

Putin would love to see the US government in shambles. China would love to see a weak United States, so they would be in a stronger bargaining position with their main trading partner.

This is what it's all really about. His niece Mary said he's "utterly incapable of leading this country." He's not supposed to lead. He's not supposed to do anything at all. Bannon promised us that his guy would take the government apart, his exact words were, "deconstruction of the administrative state." From the banking regulators to the Post Office and everything in between, from Sea to shining Sea, Big Government had to go. So here we go. First thing they had to do was get rid of all the scientists in all government agencies. No wonder there's very little help on the way from the Center for Disease Control. That's just one agency. If one hundred scientists say we need to take emergency measures to control global warming, he'll find the one crackpot who disagrees and says it's all a "cyclical" fluctuation, to fit his Chinese hoax theory.

Becoming tired of arguing with someone of inferior intellect and having already successfully gotten the Dismantler-in-Chief installed, Steve Bannon went to Europe to do his worst over there. He had so many friends there. He loves the Eurollectual Neo-Nazi crowd. Their such good Christian, nationalist, Kapitalists.

Brexit was becoming so popular amongst all the English xenophobic haters. With all the Muslims running around London wearing their traditional hijabs or even burqas, the right wing would take advantage of the one particular fear that apparently worried the Anglo-Saxon psyche more than anything else in the world: Perhaps it was the steady decline of British Fashion since the fab days of old.

The influx of Syrians and other refugees into Germany and throughout Europe combined with the sluggish economy was undermining the stability of the Union. Regardless of the cost, they would push it through, even with very little agreement between the UK and the rest of the Europeans.

Between the careless Brits and the U.S. economic woes of late, there is talk of the whole Swiss banking system collapsing, putting the Chinese on an extremely strong footing. I think they have to love Bannon, almost as much at Russia does.

The good news is our trusty moron of a leader probably really doesn't understand what Bannon wants anyway. They sort of just coexist and they've grown apart. Bannon's quite mad, actually. In all fairness it would take a team of top-notch psychiatrists to put that Humpty Dumpty back together again. From Bannon's writings, he seems to think that spanking and shaming are the cures for mental illness. I propose that it's possible he has a history of being abused, perhaps by a parent, and secretly feels the reason for his own mental frailties are intertwined with his resentment for the rejection he felt from the parent he loved. If I was his shrink, we would start by talking about his mother.

Maybe these guys want lots of people to suffer, since they're so miserable themselves. So, instead of mandating insurance coverage for mental health as Hillary advocated, it's so much cheaper to just cut Medicare and Medicaid and let people suffer. Then they'll all know how it feels to be one of *les miserables*.

There is one common thread between the 2016 and the 2020 elections. That is the Republicans are going into Election Day trailing in the polls, again.

I have been a witness to dozens and dozens of times in my lifetime that the Republicans have closed from behind and come out on top. In 1988, Bush Sr was trailing Michael Dukakis by 18 points in July until he rolled out the Willie Horton Black criminal advertisement in October. It was the most shocking blatantly racist ad that people had seen at that time. This year, we've already seen the Luis Bracamontes Mexican cop killer ad. You can be sure that's just for starters.

Usually around the weekend before the vote, they announce some scandal, unproveable in a couple of days of pandemonium, the news cycle is consumed, the narrative is usurped. Or sometimes they just outrageously besmirch immigrants or welfare recipients to summon the most polarized Republicans to the voting booths.

This time I predict they will do a double move and do both, a scandal and some unbelievable racist comments. They may even drag it out for a couple of weeks, with wave after wave of this kind of garbage. The object is to obfuscate the Democratic platform.

But this time it may not have the same effect. This time the cuckoos already represent 80% of his entire base. Also, the Democrats are not going to take the outcome for granted this time. And, by the way, when you are running from behind, you don't want to fall back 14 points in the final weeks into some sort of insurmountable death spiral.

The reason John Bolton wanted to come out with his book before the election was not because he had written a 'tell-all' with all the gory details on ex-boss and he could influence voters to vote for Biden. He hates the Democrat's guts. He wanted to sell more books.

I don't know why they're making such a big deal about Bolton's book. He is making accusations of "obstruction of justice as a way of life," as if that's supposed to be news to anybody. This madman wanted a war with Iraq that would have rivaled our debacle in Afghanistan. He dreamed of 'Bunker Buster Bombs' raining all over the place. With all those factions and zealots and civilians over there, fueled by all those zealots over here, the Tigris and Euphrates rivers would be flowing red for years and years, if Bolton's vision could come to be.

Bolton announced that he is going to write-in his vote for some conservative candidate, because he can't support either candidate. Let me help you out with your numbers Johnnie, if you vote for a third party or if you don't vote at all, just know that mathematically it amounts to one half of a vote for the one you don't like. But like a true bully, Bolton is showing his cowardice and lack of character. He can't afford to support Biden. He doesn't want his book sales to drop, let's be honest.

THE ECONOMIC OUTLOOK

This isn't over. The economy has a ton of room on the downside. I hope not, but between the huge Tax Cut for the rich, and the $4 trillion Covid giveaway package, this thing could go 'pop' really easily. Even if it doesn't (we can always print more money), the outlook is bleak.

Let's take a look at the price of gold, shall we? Up from $1,260 in 2016 to over $2,000 this August, 2020; that's up over 58%. So, your 401(k) with $200,000 in it now, can't buy you what it would have then. It's worth about $126,000 in yesterday's dollars. The weak dollar means the retirement RV you could have purchased in 2016 for $200,000 now costs $317,000 and now you can't afford it, so you're going to have to go to Plan B, a double wide in Lake Havasu, AZ and some hot dogs on the BBQ.

Larry Kudlow, the mystic business Swami from Fox is the latest lucky genius tapped to be an "economic adviser." I wonder if he just hired him, or did he have to propose the concept through Larry's agent. I wonder if he brought his own make-up artist with him; if it was part of the bundle. I wonder if he has to appear courtesy of Fox News. He follows in the footstep of dozens of "advisers". Such gems as Betsy McCaughey, Wilbur Ross's ex-wife (he just knows Wilbur so well). Most of them just come up with ideas on how to make money for themselves. Kudlow is worth a fortune, but to keep up with inflation, you know he knows he's going to need to keep growing.

His biggest contributions thus far have been pretty outlandish. I'm sure he was so impressed with himself, for coming up with the theory that unemployment compensation is a disincentive to work. I bet he thinks that was his own original philosophical masterpiece. For the 53 million Americans who have filed for unemployment so far, who are the victims of a feckless government in response to the pandemic, there haven't been that many options. And he says the benefits will be over in July. So, his big fat brainstorm was to give a $4000 tax deduction for domestic travel. Hello? It's true, so while people are lined at the food banks for miles, I can hear it now; "Oh, gee, I'm going to be evicted, I can't pay any of my bills, I was making minimum wage before (the Federal minimum is $7.25 an hour), but now I think I'll just go on vacation and write-off up to $4,000. Oh, I forgot, I don't have $4,000, oh, and I don't pay taxes anyway." So, a bunch of rich people who were going to travel anyway get another deduction. The bottom line is Kudlow is just as happy to let the government print more money which adds to the spiraling inflation.

About Covid-19, "Fatality rates continue to be very low", he said. Is that some sort of intellectualization he's using to tranquillize his own fears and anxiety? Twenty states have infection rates that are headed up sharply. Florida hit over 15,000 new cases July 12, the worst day, yet. Oh Goodness, a glimmer of hope! The moron governor, DeSantis, is advising people to consider social distancing. Ya think? No mandate for masks, though. In fact, Georgia's Governor Kemp just countermanded the mandating of wearing masks by any Georgia counties or cities (such as Atlanta). What's next, the outlawing of wearing masks? Surgeons only? Or maybe no, not even in surgery. And the new slogan can be: 'MASA - Make America Sick Again'. The President looking like a dumbbell again, made the stupid comment today in his regurgitated "China virus" briefing show, that he thinks all the governors are suggesting that, "if you want to wear a mask, you wear it." Whew! What a relief. I thought he was going to say that if you want to wear a mask, federal troops in camouflage would arrest you or mace you or beat you with clubs. No way, that only goes on in other fascist countries, not ours.

This all comes after Texas Lt. Governor Dan Patrick made his infamous speech about there being, "More important things than living." He would gladly risk his life to avert economic shutdown, he blabbered, "We got to take some risks and get back in the game, and get this country back up and running." He is some kind of frightening leader. Follow me, off a cliff! How many people have to perish before the nation comes to its senses? New cases in the US were averaging around a record 65,000 a day. Yes Larry Kudlow, you fit right in with this group of ignoramuses.

Staying more in his wheelhouse, Larry has gone back to making financial predictions again. Nobody, but nobody with any experience at all would take advise from this guy. He's always been wrong more than 50% of the time. You'd be way better off flipping a coin. He looked into the crystal ball and proclaimed, we're "off to the races" headed for a V shaped recovery.

The Republicans have been milking the good economy left to them by Democratic administrations since Bill Clinton left office. When they leave office, it's a horrible mess, as Reagan and Bush W demonstrated.

The best-case scenario is bleak. The moratorium on evictions is set to coincide with the expiration of the federal unemployment benefits this weekend. Break out the calculators: Joblessness + Homelessness + Inflation = Depression. All that's left is for the stock market to crash and there to be a run on the banks and things will get bad. A full-blown panic. So, the Senate is trying to figure out another monster giveaway, maybe this time only one or two trillion dollars, without any plan to control rampant widespread fraud like the last one. And worse, there's no plan to solve the root problems. We need job programs (contact tracers) and we need an equitable tax code. All this jerk has proposed is bringing back the deduction for the three-martini lunch. We need to overhaul the medical and pharmaceutical industries. We need to revamp our banking system and some of these gargantuan corporations are going to have to kick in. Why should millions of random people be affected, and millions of random workers become unemployed by the pandemic and bear the burden of the crushing financial losses, while others actually benefit or suffer no consequences whatsoever? If that's capitalism, it needs to be fixed.

Landlords and banks should start feeling the pain like the rest of us. There are basically two kinds of rent relief. One is you get free rent, or reduced rent for a while. The other is where you can pay what you owe later, so that the landlord gets every dime eventually, meanwhile the tenant is pushed deeper into debt. Some landlords are even waiting to take advantage of the opportunity to push tenants out who can't afford their rent-controlled apartments. Those apartments can then be rented out at new higher market rates, translating into a big windfall for landlords. So, the phony argument goes that mom and pop landlords who depend on rent from a duplex can't afford their mortgage payments and property taxes. Some are having a big problem, for sure. But most landlords can afford to give a little and are better off than most. The solution is a sliding scale allowing lower income landlords forgiveness on their mortgage, tax payments and property insurance premiums. What politicians are ready to push around the banks and giant property owners? Maybe Elizabeth Warren or Bernie, but I don't see any other leaders opening their mouths.

I predict that if gold prices don't stabilize or retract recent gains, big property owners are going to see a huge windfall, probably next year. Don't sell now.

The pandemic is made to order for Bannon and his gang. It has a glaringly worse affect on people of color, and poor people in general who receive poor medical care and therefore are in poor health. It has the effect of further escalating income inequality. The top three richest people in America now control more wealth than the bottom 50% of all Americans. The rich get richer and the poor get squashed, while the economy comes barreling down on the middle class like a freight train. What's more, they're trying to turn it into the perfect excuse for a Marshall Law takeover.

These guys act like dictators. The whole White Nationalist influence on the President is something he could get used to. He likes the idea of unchecked power. Too bad for him we have a three-branch system of government. The Executive Branch is held to answer to the Legislative Branch and to the Judicial Branch. He can wiggle around but he can't break free. He can't destroy this powerful set-up. He can talk and talk and tell us how he is omnipotent, but it only makes him look more ignorant.

Why does he hate ANTIFA so much, or was it just the distraction of the day? He wanted to have them "declared" a Terrorist Organization, but then I think he realized that in opposing them so hard, he was confessing to being a Fascist. Oh, my G-d, he was so revolting when he waxed poetic about watching the National Guard use gas to disperse protestors in Minneapolis and how it was "beautiful" like a "knife cutting through butter." Did he forget about the right of the people to peaceably assemble and the whole rest of the 1st Amendment? His favorite buddies are the Dictators in Russia, North Korea, Philippines, and Brazil. Sorry, I almost forgot Turkey.

We can't let the latest militarized defense of the Portland courthouse go untouched. He's experimenting to see if people will tolerate it. The 'Law and Order' Nixon wannabe, is thinking about a coup after the election.

Back in Berkeley in 1969, when I wasn't spending 14 hour days in the library, we used to occasionally have an anti-war rally on the Sproul Hall steps. And somebody would yell, "Let's take the park!" Then we would march down Telegraph Avenue a few blocks to People's Park. The Police would be waiting to ambush us. We would chant, "Hell No, We Won't Go," and draft cards were burned. Then some guys who nobody knew, who looked like narcs with crewcuts and blue jeans, would throw rocks at the lines of police. Then the Berkeley PD would attack the students. It happened every time. The reactionary Reagan and the fascist war-hawk Nixon loved the way it played out in the press. Nonetheless, we weren't silent, and the voices of reason were heard.

The police had jeeps ready to go, and they would drive up and down the streets blowing out teargas right and left, taking out whole blocks at a time. They were on the roofs firing rubber, and putty bullets. The Alameda County Sheriffs (we called them the 'Blue Meanies' because of their cobalt blue jumpsuits) would fire wooden bullets. They hurt, and they could break the skin.

I wore a helmet with a red cross on the top and a heavy green army jacket. I was busy passing out paper towels which I squirted with a buffer solution (compliments of the Chemistry Department) to counteract the teargas. I think the red cross must have looked like a target from the rooftops, because a lot of rounds were always bouncing all around me and I got hit a lot almost every time.

These guys in Portland are supposedly Federal U.S. Customs and Border Protection Officers (from the Oregon Border??) but you have to believe it, because they don't wear insignias. There was talk in Washington DC that some were recognized as private security personnel connected with the federal prison system. They wear camouflage or sometimes all black. They're well-armed. They attack and detain citizens, bind their hands behind their back with plastic zip ties, and put them in unmarked vehicles. I think if they aren't carrying a warrant, that it's kidnapping. They have teargas, mace and all kinds of goodies. I really have a soft spot for those protesters who brought the leaf blowers to blow the teargas back at the troops. That's my style. I used to hate those leaf blowers, but not anymore. Last night they began gassing and firing on the protesters when somebody shot fireworks at the police lines. I wonder if it was those guys who nobody knew, who looked like narcs with crewcuts and blue jeans.

The First Amendment guarantees us:

Congress shall make no law respecting an establishment of religion, or prohibiting the free exercise thereof; or abridging the freedom of speech, or of the press; or the right of the people peaceably to assemble, and to petition the Government for a redress of grievances.

This freedom is worth fighting for. We may have to resort to Civil Disobedience. The price of freedom is sometimes blood, so we have to decide if we are ready to shed blood to maintain these rights. I believe in non-violence. So, as Martin Luther King would preach, I "seek to defeat injustice", rather than people. From the day I first said the 'Pledge of Allegiance', I have been ready to stand up for America. When it comes to our rights as Americans, I accept my responsibility to be vigilant and I refuse to compromise. I wouldn't give an inch. I love my country. I support your rights. I support the rights of all Americans. When they want to arrest me, they're going to have to carry me. I'm going to do a sit-in. It wouldn't be my first.

Webster's Dictionary defines Fascism as:

> *a political philosophy, movement, or regime (such as that of the Fascisti) that exalts nation and often race above the individual and that stands for a centralized autocratic government headed by a dictatorial leader, severe economic and social regimentation, and forcible suppression of opposition*

Maybe Webster should just have a picture of the Republican President and his Attorney General.

The Greatest Generation fought against this in World War II. We won that one, didn't we?

Did you think it was over? Ever since McCarthyism and the House Un-American Activities Committee put out the Hollywood Blacklist in 1947 and the John Birch Society got their candidate Ronald Reagan elected in 1980, freedom loving people across our country have been constantly struggling to keep from letting things spiral out of control again. There's no rest for the weary. And we had better not rest.

So many times, California Governor Reagan referred to Jewish people as "you people" and again many times when he was President Reagan. Why do they make such a big deal about how the WASP-in-Chief launched his 2016 campaign in the Deep South to pander to the KKK right off the bat? Because Reagan did the same thing with his famous "States Rights" speech in Mississippi. But Reagan really was the 'Great Communicator'. Even though he was such a terrible actor, he had a knack for convincing some nasty people that they could overcome whatever vestiges of moral principles they had left and join his party. In doing so, he did more damage to our country than any person who ever lived. The myth of 'Trickle-down Economics' has persisted ever since.

Fifty years ago, California Governor Reagan destroyed the best mental health system in the world when he simply opened the doors and kicked everyone out to die in the streets. He was getting a ton of contributions from private 'board and care' facilities and the Ronnie Reagan right-wing reactionaries were all convinced that psychiatry was a big communist plot. He basically was credited with overseeing the abolishment of involuntary hospitalization. Unmedicated homelessness abounded. It's almost impossible to get someone who is mentally ill the help they so obviously need when they are too sick to cooperate. Today we have over 150,000 homeless in California and over 500,000 nationwide. Saint Reagan was truly no angel on this earth. Something is terribly wrong with his system when there are one tenth as many seriously mentally ill people in hospitals as there are behind bars. In Los Angeles alone, 40,000 people can make their choice between living in a cardboard box under the freeway, or in and out of the jail or prison system. The future isn't looking too rosy, either; the next epidemic for the United States is looking like it's going to be unemployment and homelessness. It has already been endemic for decades, but we may see a frightening jump in the numbers, and soon.

Fittingly, Reagan suffered horribly from Alzheimer' disease in the final stages of his life. Then and only then did that jewel, Nancy Reagan finally ever say something in support of people with mental illness. I would have advised her and her beloved Ronnie to go live in an underpass somewhere.

One major contribution that will always be attributed to Ronald Reagan was that, for the purposes of meeting the requirements of the school lunch program, ketchup was to be considered a vegetable. What a kind and benevolent ruler, he was. Reagan's appointment of James Watt to be Secretary of the Interior was an eye-opener for me. I guess I was naïve. I couldn't believe that the anti-environmentalist, who sued the Federal government to advocate for the Power companies, would be in charge of protecting the environment. Strip-mine the National Parks, shall we?

Reagan led the way, what a horrid trailblazer. But now we have the disciple. This indolent slob really has done virtually nothing good whatsoever his whole term. I don't think he even thinks he has. Except for to ruin the Federal courts with the reckless appointments he's made, nothing at all. Great golfing.

When Hurricane Maria slammed into Puerto Rico in 2017, he treated the more than three million American residents there as if he were some kind of a benevolent stranger giving them charity. Does he remember that those are taxpaying citizens and they were depending on their government to come through for them in an emergency. He behaved like a jester throwing rolls of paper towels out to the crowd; and that was symbolic of what? It showed his lack of compassion for the 3,000 to 4,600 people that were killed. He claimed the federal response was an "incredible success" and that only from six to eighteen deaths had occurred. "If a person died for any reason, like old age, just add them to the list," he chirped. Yeah right, like deaths related to power outages at the hospital in Manati, no fresh water, no refrigerated foods, no critical medicines. That's the federal response, which was no response, the way he likes it, with a good funny photo-op to boot.

CHAPTER **7**

Analysis

This is a man who doesn't think in terms of polls, he thinks in terms of ratings. It's pretty predictable for a show business professional. He knows about what people like to watch on TV. He likes to watch TV and he knows what he likes.

He must feel as though his family has been under siege by the government since he can remember. He comes from a long line of criminals. His father was a big contractor and developer in New York and very well connected. The son of a Gold Rush pimp, Fred was accused of profiteering off of federal and state real estate projects in the 1950's and 1960's. His ties to organized crime are possibly the subject of his highly redacted FBI file. Information about his $350,000 campaign donation to NY Mayor Ed Koch, was not redacted.

As his son started running things, he was forever getting into hot water over Civil rights and building code violations.

Through his construction endeavors and Atlantic City Casino, he had connections with all kinds of mobsters like "Fat Tony" Salerno, boss of the Genovese crime family. He somehow avoided problems building his Towers in NY when the whole concrete workers union was on strike. It's said that nothing got built in NY without Salerno getting a cut. I really have nothing positive to say about them, but at least I could say they were well organized. The point is he learned a deep-seated contempt for the law throughout his life.

Where does hate come from? Any examination of this guy without an in-depth discussion of the subject would be incomplete. It reveals the basis of the unshakable strength he has with his followers. For me, hate is the opposite of what my mother taught me. She told me about love for life, people, and the beautiful world we lived in. Maybe his parents lacked those few basic traits that left him wounded and undeveloped in many respects with feelings of bitterness and a jaundiced outlook (no that's not why he's orange). What family dynamics may have led to the enmity between him and his father causing further unsatiated feelings, frustrations and fear of failure?

Envy is a dangerous feeling that can evolve from an inferiority complex. Although it seems contradictory, good financial fortune does not necessarily insulate us from envious desires. In fact, sometimes enough is never enough. Coupled with jealousy of the perceived stature of another, a low self-esteem can morph into insecurity and resulting anxiety. Quite often it spawns from rudimentary perceptions of unfairness. Then retribution fills the logical gap, and before you know it, you can plead not guilty by reason of insanity.

Now, as if one hateful heart wasn't bad enough, comes the phenomenon of group hate. People are able to form strong bonds through their common hatred for another person or group. Particularly when they are resentful and dissatisfied with their lives and looking for someone to blame besides themselves. By sharing their authentic feelings with other people, they gain each other's trust and empathy (did I say 'empathy' in relation to this monster with ice-water in his veins?). Let's say they bond together in something resembling friendship that reinforces the commitment they have expressed, to ideas that they often know are wrong or evil.

This concept in leadership, of hate and division has been repeated over and over for thousands of years. The right-wing has just brought it forward into the 21st century. Weaponized by computers and massive socio-economic disfunction, they can spread discord far and wide.

Still, the rest of us have them outnumbered. They aren't able to make the headway they think they deserve. Unfortunately, that only leads to frustration and further anxiety. A typical co-morbidity found with up to half of all anxiety disorders is depression.

A Borderline Personality Disorder (BPD), otherwise known as an Emotionally Unstable Personality Disorder (EUPD) is diagnosed through [1] a pervasive pattern of failed interpersonal relationships ("you're fired"), low self-image, affects, and [2] marked impulsivity (30,000 tweets, 468 in one week 06/04/2020).

He publicly exhibits his Sadistic Personality Disorder (SPD) when he gets pleasure from causing pain to others. Clear examples are stealing of children from immigrants, or forcing descendants of slaves to endure statues and flags honoring the practice of slavery.

The pandemic is taking a toll on the President, both politically and psychologically. His advisors are telling newspapers that he is developing a "woe-is me attitude," and that he is "confounded" by events. He recently made a confidential visit to Walter Reed National Military Hospital, for an undisclosed reason. Then he made the revelation on Fox that he had undergone a mental status exam. He confessed, "I actually took one when I uh very recently when I, uh, when I was – you know the radical left was saying, is he all there, is he all there? And I proved I was all there because I aced it. I aced the test. And he should take the same exact test." He was referring to Joe Biden. "A very standard test. I took it at Walter Reed Medical Center in front of doctors, and they were very surprised. They said, that's an unbelievable thing. Rarely does anybody do what you just did."

There are many basic mental status exams. They are usually short and can be extremely simple. Examples of basic questions or tasks that are often given are.

What year is it?

Draw the numbers on a clock.

Repeat this phrase: 'No ifs, ands, or buts.'

Count backwards from 100 by sevens (serial sevens).

What is this? A watch. A pencil.

A doctor would administer such an exam to screen a patient for a suspected case of dementia. Not to screen for the patient's competency to be the leader of the free world. If one is the President, and one is worried that one might need this type of mental exam, one should resign immediately, and then go take one's tests.

The diagnosis of Major Depressive Disorder requires 2 weeks of depressed mood, or loss of interest in activities, plus 4 of the following symptoms:

- sleep disorders (nightly insomnia or hypersomnia),
- unintended weight change (gain or loss),
- psychomotor agitation or retardation,
- fatigue or reduced energy,
- feelings of worthlessness or guilt,
- difficulty concentrating and processing information, and
- thoughts of death or suicide.

How do you think this morbidly obese, all night tweeter, who can't think, and moves around like a sloth got like that?

The diagnosis of Generalized Anxiety Disorder requires too much anxiety or worry for 6 months and an inability to manage it, plus 3 of the following symptoms:

- restlessness (feeling keyed up or on edge),
- tires easily or fatigue,
- difficulty concentrating,
- irritability,
- muscle tension,
- sleep disturbance (difficulty falling asleep, staying asleep or unsatisfying sleep)

Look at him, he's like the 'poster boy'.

The good news for him is that these two conditions both respond well to serotonin norepinephrine reuptake inhibitors

(SNRI's). I wouldn't be surprised if he was currently on some regimen including duloxetine, or desvenlafaxine. Or maybe he'd react beautifully to some good old-fashioned Zoloft, a selective serotonin reuptake inhibitor (SSRI). These drugs work by interfering with the normal degradation of naturally occurring chemicals in the brain. They are the important chemicals that contribute to feelings of well-being and happiness. I don't think there's any reason to fear that there would be any drug interactions with his hydroxychloroquine malaria treatment that he says he likes to take sometimes. If we had to knock out one of them due to the combination causing possible undesirable cardiac effects, such as serotonin syndrome, it would definitely have to be the hydroxychloroquine.

The Apprentice TV show was a real hoot. He got to act like a mean jerk who knew-it-all, and people loved it. "You're Fired" he said to them all one at a time as ratings remained good. When you watched that show, you felt that if those people could make it that far, you could make it that far. Gary Busey made it. As long as you kissed up to the boss, and didn't hurt the ratings, you made it. Would the ruthless, back-stabbing Black contestant make it to the next round? Stay tuned to find out. He was becoming famous for being powerful, a double whammy. What a dream come true.

Freud teaches that the unconscious feelings influence rational thought. Narcissistic personality disorder is characterized by increased self-importance, a need to be envied, and a profound lack of empathy. This diagnosis, almost every psychiatrist agrees, hits the nail on the head. "Only I can fix it," he said about the country. Predictably, people who suffer from NPD usually will not admit it. His feelings of omnipotence, Freud reasoned, are an acknowledgement of vestiges of the megalomania of infancy.

To put it simply, like a big baby who is proud of the power he has to control people. "I'm the greatest President ever." The little baby would say, "Wah wah wah. Respect me. I don't care about you, but I know you care about me."

NPD is perhaps one of his most dangerous personality deficiencies. When coupled with self-appreciation of his ineffective rhetorical style to handle a tough question, he can fly off the handle and deride a reporter or the news outlet they work for instead. We really don't know how much we are depending on cooler heads to prevail, when he can't keep up with other world leaders and flips out on them.

One of his first calls was to the Prime Minister of Australia, Malcolm Turnbull, where the President lost it and began talking about how Obama made a disgusting deal to accept a couple of thousand refugees, and he didn't like it. He told the Prime Minister that the conversation was "crazy" and cut short the call and publicly said it was "the worst call by far". And that's Australia, one of our solid allies.

Projection, one of his persistent defense mechanisms, lets him say about others what he fears are his own deficiencies. A quick example is warning that the Democrats are going to try to cheat and steal the election, when that is what he's planning to do, as probably the only way he can win.

He uses irrational behavior to deny his guilt. He has botched the response to the pandemic, if he ever tried to mount a response at all. So, he pleads incompetency by saying something outrageous (nobody thinks you should inject Lysol, or thinks decreased testing would be beneficial and lead to decreased daily cases), so he can act like a sympathetic victim. He's the victim of one witch-hunt after another.

He has caused a deeper divide in the country than any President ever. People can't even just be friends, anymore. It's even hard to do business with someone, across party lines. In all my 35 years in business, I've always been able to deal with people without regard to political ideology. There's more to it than that now. It's been elevated to differences in moral ideology. The profound divergence in levels of basic decency obliterates the respect that people can have for one another.

His extreme views leave no room for compromise. He thinks in extremes, no room for middle ground. No room for a middle class, either. We're rich and you're not. Deal with it.

He can go into a tirade of unhinged unconnected thoughts at any time. He struggles to express his thoughts. He wants to go off script. He wants to act like himself on the off chance that he may say something good, and people will like him for who he really is. The problem is that would be the rare case. It's much more likely that his thoughts will be very hateful, ridiculous, and full of word salad, wrong words, and repetitions.

In December 2019, a group of 350 psychiatrists and other health professionals signed on to a troubling report regarding the effects of the impeachment proceedings on the President. Doctors from Yale University, George Washington University and other top professionals including a former CIA profiler, concluded that he was a "threat to the safety our nation." They were alarmed by the rapid deterioration of his mental health.

Interestingly, the American Psychiatric Association adopted the "Goldwater rule" when Republican Arizona Senator Barry Goldwater ran against Lyndon Johnson in 1964. Psychiatrists had agreed that he was not fit to become President. The rule prohibited psychiatrists from making public statements about the mental health of public figures unless they had personally examined them. But this was in conflict with their other guidelines, which specifically obligated psychiatrists to educate the public when asked about a public figure to protect the community, thus using medical science for the betterment of mankind. Goldwater was a crackpot right-wing reactionary card-carrying member of the John Birch Society. People used to be concerned that a lunatic like that might get his fingers on our nuclear weapons arsenal. Also, the Geneva Declaration of the World Medical Association (of 1948) mandated physicians to identify mental illnesses when there were serious humanitarian reasons. This edict was declared in response to the tragic lessons of WWII in the era of the Nuremburg Trials.

The 2019 petition went on to state that he has exhibited "brittleness of his sense of worth. Any slight criticism is experienced as a humiliation and degradation. To cope with the resultant hollow and empty feeling, he reacts with what is referred to as narcissistic rage. He is unable to take responsibility for any error, mistake, or failing. His default in that situation is to blame others and to attack the perceived source of his humiliation. These attacks of narcissistic rage can be brutal and destructive."

The lead psychiatrist commented that he is "doubling and tripling down on his delusions," ramping up on his conspiracy theories, with "a great deal of cruelty and vindictiveness," and that the tweets were accelerating and repetitive. They were thought to "fit the pattern of delusions, rather than just plain lies."

Well, at first glance, you might ask yourself why it should take 8 years of medical school and a lifetime of practice to notice those traits in the President. We all know the problem as if anyone could see right through him. But now we can understand why he is powerless to act any differently. The defense of his own ego is going to rule the day. He's weak, and he's never been required to control his emotional outbursts. In fact, like a clown, he is gratified by public laughter at his vulgarity and hateful wisecracks.

The petition soon grew to 773 signatures. Can I sign it?

His niece has a Ph.D. in psychology. She compares him to a 3-year old in her new book, "Too Much and Never Enough." She diagnoses him as a "high-functioning sociopath" following in his father's footsteps. She says she often heard him use the 'N' word and anti-Semitic slurs. That's sure following in his father's footsteps. I guess everyone would be surprised if a Klansman used those words, too. She blames her grandfather, for driving her father, the President's brother, to alcoholism.

The big difference between a sociopath and a psychopath is that a psychopath is more calculating and is unable to form genuine emotional attachments. They are manipulative and sometimes able to hold down a job or a shallow relationship or family for years, even though they lack empathy. Sociopaths are thought to be more easily irritated and can lash out in volatile fits of rage. In his case I think the difference is rather moot, due to his position and fame, but if I had to pick one, I would classify him as a psychopath. They are thought to be less remorseful, and more calculating and meticulous and design their evil plans, complete with variations for all contingencies. Also, the psychopath is more likely to inherit their underdeveloped brains as opposed to the sociopath typically evolving from an abusive childhood. It is possible to have a combination of both of these two antisocial personality disorders; there are a lot of crossovers in the profiles of the patient's signs and symptoms. People who show a reckless disregard for the safety of others, or for themselves, can generally fit into either category.

This brain damaged social pariah has a degree from Wharton. I find it practically impossible to believe he ever graduated from nursery school. Not legitimately anyway. I really can't imagine him trying to read a book, at any point in his life. He consults his own brain for wisdom, and he has said as much many times. "I have the best words," he says. He can't say the word 'origins' he says oranges. Another tongue-twister, 'Yosemite' comes out as Yo-Semite.

He declared in 2016 that he was his own best foreign policy advisor because, "I'm speaking with myself, number one, because I have a very good brain, and I said a lot of things." Tell me about the rabbits, George, this guy is a blithering idiot. Sorry, that is insulting terminology, let me rephrase; he has an intellectual disability.

CHAPTER 8

Epilogue

So many people have become inspired to work to move back towards putting our country back together again. Americans love their country because there really is something here worthy of their commitment. We are free to live the lives we choose as long as we don't interfere with the rights of others. America is a gorgeous land of stunning natural landscapes, and amazing cities. The people are inclined to be very friendly and we are famous for our Yankee ingenuity. We will work together to prevail.

It is so entertaining to watch former Republicans do their song and dance about how they don't support the emperor (anymore). It's like they've discovered the wheel. Suddenly the Democrats make sense. And they are so eloquent in their criticism as if they were born liberal. They're funny and everything, but I just don't forgive that easily. Sorry Michael Steele, former RNC chairperson, but I don't trust you. You criticize the buffoon real hard, but you were a sellout before, and you aren't that committed. Sorry Nicole Wallace, you are very empathetic, but you were Bush's Communications person and I bet you loved it when he appointed Samuel Alito to the Supreme Court. I know you can't get behind President Bozo, but would you stand up for the poor and oppressed people of the world? I'm just not getting that feeling that you're an eco-terrorist tree-hugger like me.

And this Lincoln Project with founders like Rick Wilson and Steve Schmidt, you know they're going to represent the old Republican guard and leave the President without leg to stand on. They have raised many millions of dollars to produce political ads to mostly point to his various personality disorders rather than his political shortcomings. Some ads are funny, but don't forget this clown likes it when you laugh at him, even when he gets mad, he's relishing the attention. Their humor lacks political bite, because if the subject of the joke was a ruse, a distraction to avoid an unfriendly news cycle, then the jokes on you. And that's often been the case.

And that Schmidt is inordinately articulate, and his cutting rhetoric is really deep. I like it very much. He is a genius for sure, but again, he also was some kind of a genius when he was a Republican strategist, too. George W Bush and Arnold Schwarzenegger are the punishments he inflicted on both the nation and the state that I love, and I guess I am cursed with an impeccable memory like a steel trap about things like that.

The only hope for our battered nation is Education. Because voters can't figure out what's going on without it. Education. Don't leave home without it. As an example, how do you notice that inflation is decimating your nest egg, when you're clipping along at about a 2nd grade level of math skills. I want to tell you, or I should tell you, that most Americans can't figure out 7 x 9. When their cellphone runs out of power, they are dead in the water. There's not even a fundamental level of understanding of Geography, any Foreign Language, or much if any Science knowledge. It's sad but true. And forget Civics, a lot of them know as much about the workings of government as the Church tells them they need to know to get Roe *v.* Wade overturned, which is: Vote for Mitch McConnell. You can't make an informed decision, when you are ill-informed.

We need to make sure that people who want to continue on with higher learning have the opportunity. At least we could make tuition affordable for all. I don't see the benefit of an all-expense paid life for every student, and then for them to be stuck with a massive bill to repay for the next 20 years. Tuition needs to be cut or eliminated altogether, especially for economically disadvantaged students. A free ride with room and board should be reserved for only the most qualified students who otherwise would not be able to afford to go full time.

And everybody has to stop having so many kids. Especially if you can't afford them. There can be no educational system, no medical system, no decent sustainable environment, no hope, if every family has 10 kids, and their kids have 10 kids and so on, and so on…. Pick a number, 2 kids, 4 kids, 5 kids, but at least let's pick some maximum allowable number and stick to it. Nobody wants to tell other people what to do, but there is simply not an alternative. Either we can all be miserable, or we can put a lid on the problem. How many times in Los Angeles have you seen them add 3 more lanes to the freeway in both directions? It just turns into 14 lanes of daily traffic jam. California is becoming one big cement parking lot. Many other areas of the country are just as bad or worse.

We should be leading the world in trying to save the environment. Instead our leader sits silently when Brazil's leader, madman Jair Bolsonaro oversees the destruction of the Amazon rain forest. Aside from the elimination of human rights for the indigenous people there, the deforestation is up by 88% according to wildlife watchdogs, using satellite technology. Brazilian scientists even admit to a 50% increase in the first quarter of 2020. This is the same dictator who said he would no longer release Covid-19 hospitalization numbers in the wake of criticism over runaway explosion of the coronavirus across Brazil. Maybe he wants to be number one in the world in something else besides soccer. It's a real foot race with the USA enjoying a comfortable lead, but you know how quickly this virus spreads when you stop trying to contain it.

Now it turns out that Bolsonaro has tested positive for the virus. The fool who never wears a mask and is constantly meeting with people who aren't wearing masks, contracted the infection, he calls it "mold in his lungs," and it's his wife that's testing positive for Covid-19. Now we have to figure out what's next. Either he must be very ill, otherwise he never would have admitted catching it, or he doesn't have it at all, and wants to prove how tough he is, and how easily the disease resolves. It's pretty disgusting either way. Maybe what comes around, goes around, after all. Maybe it will make people more cautious and the curve will level out a bit in Brazil.

The United States needs to get signed back on to the Paris Agreement. The good news is, the rest of the world has not quit fighting just because the U.S. dropped out. And combustion engine usage is down really substantially worldwide lately due to self-imposed mobility restrictions resulting from fear of the virus. The skies are relatively clean and so beautiful. I heard someone in India actually could see the Taj Mahal, wow! Los Angeles has mountains, nobody knew that. So great let's build on that Mr. Biden and get serious about conservation (not to ever be confused with conservatism). My grandchildren are going to need a place to raise their families one day. I am willing to make sacrifices for this. Let's all change our way of living and clean up our own messes.

I drive the coolest car. Forget your car, my car is cooler. My car runs on hydrogen. Water (H_2O) comes out of the tailpipe, that's all. They make the hydrogen in the most environmentally friendly way possible which is currently with natural gas. But theoretically, it could be made from solar power, windmills, or even the motion of the tides. I'm a "pioneer" according to Toyota. The state of California likes the idea so much, they gave me a check for $5,000 (my state is cooler than your state, too). I think they got the money from selling pollution 'Carbon Credits'. But I also got a free $15,000 credit card, which is only good to buy hydrogen, but it's good for 3 years (I have a 3-year lease) and I'll never use it all. The interior is beautiful, it is loaded with everything, $400 a month, and it's pretty fast.

I cannot understand why people would vote for this filthy slob, who promised he would allow the coal industry to continue making a huge, big, giant mess. They have to drive their big macho pickup trucks; one person commuting in a big truck, 14 miles per gallon, tailgating everyone in their way. I can't figure out the problem with these people, unless they just never learned that they need to clean up after themselves. There's a whole new concept that they just don't understand: It's called 'other people'.

Global warming is the elephant in the room. The greenhouse gasses, like carbon dioxide and methane, trap heat from the sun. As the earth's temperature goes up, if the ocean warms by even one degree, the polar icecaps start to melt. Right now, big ships are regularly traversing through the Arctic Circle every summer. This is something that was impossible a couple of decades ago, except by special massive ships called 'Icebreakers'. Suddenly, new ports are popping up in Northern Canada, Alaska, Russia, Scandinavia and Greenland as very big and small freighters are traipsing all over the Arctic Ocean.

Without our icecaps, the earth absorbs more heat from the sun because the ice and snow reflected 90% of incoming rays, but water absorbs 90% of it. We need the ice to stabilize our weather, earthquakes, and keep our sea level from rising. Things are heating up quickly.

We may need ice more than we know. It may be a key to stabilize the rotation and axis and even the orbit of the planet. Think of a hard-boiled egg in the shell, spinning freely on a countertop. Then imagine a raw egg in the shell spinning, but quickly starting to wobble. That's just my own unverified hypothesis.

Unless we reduce greenhouse gas emissions, current projections point to a 1.5 degree increase already locked in, about one half of a degree higher than we are already measuring. The Paris Agreement goals of a maximum of 1.5 degrees Centigrade above preindustrial levels could result in a sea level rise 5 feet by the year 2100 with some models estimating a lot higher. This could displace 10's of millions of people from coastal areas, if not more.

Some people argue that we shouldn't worry about things hundreds or thousands of years in the future. First of all, who do we think we are, to destroy our beautiful world? But we need to also worry about the near-term future, because things have a way of getting out of control and growing exponentially, and we might get to witness our own destruction, as some experts warn. We don't want to live with crop shortages, water supplies destroyed, giant tsunamis, the earth uninhabitable; we don't want to live as if on the set of a science fiction disaster movie.

We can be smart and reduce greenhouse gas levels. But we need leaders to guide us through the process. Not by Republicans to represent businesses that only care about the profit margin. No! Mitt Romney, corporations are not people. And if you think so, you can go star in a science fiction movie because you're not a person either. And the Supreme Court can be your screenwriters.

Another enemy of the planet is Representative Jim Jordan, the Ohio Republican was the first to sign the No Climate Tax pledge to prove that he could care less about CO2, or other greenhouse gases. The always very nasty and sharp-tongued muscle-head was elected by Ohio voters primarily for his ability as a wrestler and for going to some Law School, without passing the bar. Just kidding, they love him so much because his district, Ohio's 4th, has been gerrymandered to resemble a snake that was run over by a truck (or maybe a seahorse?). He wouldn't want to face the voters of Cleveland, Toledo, or Columbus, but they might re-cut it again. His district is so solid, he's been winning his elections by almost double every time. There's plenty of room to try to split some Republican support off to an adjoining district if necessary. They already hold 12 out of the 16 seats, but things could get worse for them this time around, and the Republicans run the state legislature.

He is a brown-noser for the President and fawns all over his every ridiculous word. He knows what side his bread is buttered on, a real Republican through and though. He's a very reliable vote for those that have bought and paid for him. He's going to be there for a while. He's not qualified to do anything else, and Ohio voters are so backwards. I hope if the globe starts getting too warm, he has a good antiperspirant, so he can keep on working in his shirtsleeves, his trademark.

The largest of five giant offshore accumulations of plastic is the Great Pacific Garbage Patch in the Pacific Ocean between California and Hawaii. It is estimated at over 600,000 square miles and 80,000 tons. 75% of the mass of the patch is comprised of chunks bigger than 2 inches. There's more garbage there, then all the garbage that has come out of all the Fox commentators' mouths combined, so far.

It is estimated that two million tons of plastic flow into the ocean just through rivers every year. But it's the fishing industry that's the major contributor to this mess. I remember, one day, seeing a big tangled mess of lines, nets and ropes on my absolute favorite beach in Hawaii, at Kailua Beach Park. It was all twisted up with barnacles and seaweed rolled up in it. It was about 3 to 4 feet in diameter and was like a hundred feet long. I don't know if it was later removed, or if the tide came back up and reclaimed it.

A lot of marine life ends up ingesting this plastic. Sea turtles, albatross chicks and hundreds of other species can build up harmful levels of toxins from the large quantities they eat. People can build up these toxins as they eat the contaminated fish with very unhealthy outcomes. Entanglement is another unfortunate reality for many marine mammals, fish, birds and other sea life when they become inescapably snared by 'ghost nets'.

Another giant threat to our oceans is the insane idea of drilling for oil at sea. This idiocy has been going on for well over 120 years. In California I remember going surfing in Goleta, which is near Santa Barbara in 1968 and coming back with tar all over my feet. That was the year Union Oil had 'discovered' the Dos Cuadras tract. Then soon after was the 1969 oil spill disaster in the Santa Barbara channel. That didn't take long. What the heck, they made lots of money anyway, who cares about 35 miles of some of most gorgeous coastline in the world.

When the Exxon-Valdez spilled 750,000 barrels of oil all over the magnificent Prince William Sound in Alaska in 1989, it was only the 54th biggest spill in history. British Petroleum dwarfed that with a 4.9-million-barrel spill in 2010. The well exploded and oil started blasting out 5,100 feet deep below sea level. The Coast Guard searched courageously, but 11 of the 105 men on the rig were never found. The cleanup went on for years. Considered the worst marine environmental disaster in history, BP got away by paying $18 billon in fines, $65 billion altogether including cleanup costs and damages. A valiant effort was mounted to mitigate their damages. So the cost was still just a mere blip on their balance sheet.

The entire Gulf of Mexico and the Caribbean was affected by the spill that had gone on for five months before the well could be capped. Fish and wildlife are still trying to recover 10 years later and may never fully recover. Irreplaceable wetlands and estuaries were ruined. Louisiana, Mississippi, Alabama, and Florida coastlines, beaches and businesses were completely taken out.

I decided to research a little to see what the finger pointing was all about. Cost cutting and defective cement was blamed on BP, Transocean, and, lo and behold, our old friend Haliburton. Where Haliburton is, Dick Cheney couldn't be far behind. He was their CEO from 1995 to 2000 when he became George W's Vice President. The Deepwater Horizon drilling rig was completed in March 2000. Then he got $20 million when he left Haliburton.

Dick Cheney was the VP who got a heart transplant in 2012. He wanted to live long enough to make sure nobody else could get healthcare. Especially not affordable healthcare or single payer healthcare. But he was a big anti-environmentalist who never met a pipeline he didn't like.

Meanwhile, in Los Angeles, in Culver City, the Howard Hughes Center was completed in the year 2000. Acres of precious wetlands were plowed under. It was built against the 405 freeway on the Hughes Helicopter property and contained a Prominade (mall), offices, and big corporate headquarters for entertainment giants like Sony and Univision. Ballona Creek, which was a cement storm drain by now, as far down as the Ballona Wetlands Ecological Reserve, ran all the way to the Pacific Ocean. When they built the Center, they had to promise that the rest of the creek, about five miles, all the way to the Pacific, was dedicated to remain pristine wetlands for eternity. Then when they built Playa Vista, thousands of apartments, condos, and stores all the way down to Lincoln Blvd, they promised that the rest of the creek, about two miles, all the way to the Pacific, was dedicated to remain pristine wetlands for eternity (yes, that's a copy and paste). It was historically a big drainage basin for Los Angeles, fed by cienegas (swamps) and many tributaries long ago destroyed by development. Now it is supplied by rainwater and other runoff. But like so many places in the world, it was part of a delicate ecosystem. It was certainly a very nice place if you were a bird. And particularly before the City of Los Angeles and its century of business minded City Councilpersons started selling all kinds of permits. It's a different world, today. The residents of Playa Vista have waged a constant battle against methane gas and even radon gas. Release valves have been installed all over the many developments to prevent the gasses from building up to explosive and toxic levels. Expensive methane gas detectors and exhaust systems have been mandated to protect the area, now. Good lookin' out, LA City Council!

To a large extent, we make the world we live in.

That's a big reason why I'm so excited about the Destroyer-in-Chief beckoning the end of the Republican Party. A lot of the people I talk to say if we get rid of him, even the coronavirus plague was worth it. I don't like to think of it in terms of one or the other. The windbag President says the Democrats don't want the virus to resolve, that we want the pandemic to continue, to keep the economy from boosting him up for re-election. I will be so happy to see him fall on his face. We need to keep up the positive energy so we can work our way out of this mess. There's a ton of work to do, and we need to flatten the resistance if we're ever going to make it. Let's all be relentless until we achieve the world we are looking for.

Black Lives Matter and Covid-19 are among two of his recent examples of colossal blundering and mismanagement. His Approval Ratings have never been much lower, now around 40%. They are separate issues yet very inextricably connected.

Minorities in this country are at risk of experiencing more serious complications from the virus due to a higher prevalence of health problems, like diabetes and heart disease, coupled with the inferior medical care they receive. In fact, while African Americans make up 14% of the population, they account for 40% of Covid related deaths.

When there is Medicare for All, health outcomes will move towards equality, and mortality rates can begin to coincide.

But how can we ignore the manifest interconnectivity of so many issues such as wider opportunities in education, the economy, LGBTQ discrimination, immigration, the environment, racism, and everything from gun control to police reform, Covid-19, and medical care. These concerns are interrelated in so many ways.

For instance, gun sales are up like crazy since the virus outbreak. The virus has disrupted the justice systems, jury trials have been severely limited in Los Angeles, and all over the world, and courts are just beginning to reopen on a limited basis. Black Lives Matter marches can leave the streets full of broken glass and graffiti in their wake. Everybody sees the connection to the economy, here, right? Nobody in their right mind condones looting or other violence, by any means, but we can easily understand where its coming from. People are sick of it. I'm White and I'm sick of it. But right now, it's not about me. This is about my Black brothers and sisters, and I am here to tell you that I will stick up for them every single time. Black lives matter, so don't forget the people who have needlessly suffered unimaginable pain and be there for them.

Instead of trying to lead, he recently retweeted a scene from a golf cart parade in a retirement community called The

Villages, in Florida, showing a man shouting "white power" at protesters. Of course, he claimed he didn't look at it. He often puts something out there for his most deviant followers, and then pulls it back, or contradicts himself to hide behind the opposite position later. It was so clear, ten seconds into the clip, an idiot raising his fist, yelling "white power" clear as a bell. The President is championing racism. It's insane. He needs to go. No more "take backs".

Police brutality is happening everywhere; every big city, every small department, one place worse than the other. I totally disagree with those that say that most peace officers are decent, wonderful, and blah, blah, blah. Ask yourself this question: Out of 100 sworn Police Officers, how many of them would testify against another Officer? Don't tell me there's no such thing as a blue wall of silence. Or how many of them would lie on the stand to put a "bad guy" away? How many would illegally entrap a "bad guy"? Which side are the bad guys? With all their little toys they love to play with, they inflict pain routinely. These are the ones about whom the teacher used to report, "Doesn't play well with others." Maybe just a little extra click or two on the handcuffs. Or a nice dig on the back of the neck with some small device. It's torture, un-American, so wrong, and the public doesn't deserve it, and the public is supposedly the ones they serve. This is not a minor problem; if you notice there are tens of thousands of people showing up for the protest rallies all over the country and all over the world. It's no wonder one hundred thousand people showed up on Hollywood Blvd in Los Angeles, because this is a pervasive problem. Because it happens to them, to anyone and everyone. This country is turning into a police state, and people aren't going to accept it.

And it takes somebody with his hands in his pockets crushing the life out of George Floyd, and a couple people catching it on their cell phones before anyone pays attention. Suppose you were there that day in Minneapolis: What if you went up and shoved that policeman off of his neck and saved that man's life? I would gladly come visit you in state prison, if you lived long enough to make it to trial.

There is no accountability, if you complain about abuse, you're lucky if you don't get sued for libel or slander. Don't waste your time, mostly your complaints go nowhere. Even with video. These Police Unions are outrageous. They defend anything; every case to the hilt. There needs to be laws limiting these Unions. Not about wages, but about discipline for brutality. 30 days of desk duty is not a punishment. It's a vacation. Demotion, suspension, expulsion, those are punishments. There also obviously needs to be a lower threshold to block a fired officer from being hired by another (sometimes neighboring) agency. A threshold below Murder 2. Maybe 3 strikes your out. They love throwing that at citizens, so turnabout is fair play. How about 3 complaints, you can go sell hot dogs, or whatever else you're qualified for (apologies to hot dog vendors) after some time served?

And I don't put the Prosecutors on a high pedestal either. How often do they get a plea deal by threatening innocent defendants with lengthy sentences? How often do they induce stool pigeon witnesses or cellmates to give false testimony, by offering a reduced sentence deal for them in exchange for the perjury?

The Judges are no saints, sorry. They're some of the worst, many coming up through the ranks. They are the operators of the cash registers of the justice system. People are sick of that, too. The court should work for us, not the other way around. For one thing it's time to give it a rest with the traffic stop checkpoints where a line of tow trucks waits to steal people's cars and come back for more, holding them for ransom for the crime of no license or registration. This is such a blatant move; they even compensate the administrating police districts with tens of thousands of dollars for a single day event. And unconstitutional? Not if a judge signs off on it.

Probable cause gets its power from the 4th Amendment to the U.S. Constitution:

> *"The right of the people to be secure in their persons, houses, papers, and effects, against unreasonable searches and seizures, shall not be violated, and no Warrants shall issue but upon probable cause..."*

Unchecked searches are done in other countries, not ok in our country. I don't appreciate Peace Officers looking into my car window, to see if they can spot a violation to make some money for their municipality. Not my seat belts, not my cell phones, not my hair style, not my clothes, or ethnicity or race. If you work for me, you can just go solve some crimes, and leave good citizens alone. Go write some citations for failure to wear a mask. I don't need you to protect me with your radar speed guns, and I am offended by your frisking people to find evidence against them, using the pretext that you were making sure they weren't armed (those are two different types of searches). If I'm weaving all over the road, or driving dangerously, that's a different story, but if you need a radar detector to tell the difference, then get off of my case. Anyway, that's what I learned back in my first-year law school days, before I dropped out. The President never went to law school either, I guess that's pretty obvious.

I wish I could believe that was the worst of it, but so much is going on in the courts and behind the scenes, it's frightening. And on top of the food chain are the private for-profit prisons. Always needing fresh victims and trying to hold on to the ones they've got. They never complain about overcrowding, they call it growth.

It's time to reform the Police and it's time for an overhaul of the whole justice system. For one thing, I think about 25% of the people currently incarcerated could be released with some of them going to 'outpatient drug programs' and some just straight up 'let go' so they could go home to the people that love them. Not saying to let the bad guys go, but the other ones. 25% of State and Federal prisoners alike could be cut out, time served. We'd save a fortune. Incarceration costs over $80,000 per inmate per year, and almost double that for juveniles.

But let's not do it for the money. Let's not do it just because the prison system is a cesspool of coronavirus making conditions tantamount to cruel and unusual punishment. Let's do it because our justice system stinks, and the sentences are too long resulting in punishments that are way out of line with the crimes.

The only time you hear the Republicans complaining about prison costs, is when they're trying to justify the death penalty. A death penalty case always costs the taxpayers a minimum of $500,000, and sometimes much, much more than that, so there goes that argument. On that subject, no criminal was ever deterred by fear of the death penalty. They might rethink about committing a crime, because somebody could get killed, and that's further than they want to go, but not for the fear of being executed. A life sentence has been shown to be a more effective deterrent, in one study after another. In 2020, the racial disparity that remains at every level of the justice systems is palpable. It can be found all along the capital punishment process. From policing to the charging process to sentencing, studies show the system is severely tilted. Juries are the worst. The selection process is biased, and the verdicts are skewed when the defendant is Black. Police lie on the witness stand and manufacture evidence time after time. The police motto is: 'You lie to it; I'll swear to it.' And while half of all murder victims are Black, 80% of all death penalties were handed down when the victim was white. Explain that. You can't, because those numbers are too significant.

We are only human, and we make mistakes. Look at this big mouth President who took out full page advertisements in New York newspapers calling for the execution of the Central Park Five. It's a famous case from 1989, where five Black youths were sent to prison for assault and rape. These children confessed under questioning without a lawyer present. They were found to have been questioned under coercive circumstances. The semen evidence collected was from only one attacker. DNA evidence exonerated the convictions when, in 2001, a convicted murderer confessed to the rape, and his DNA was a match. The 16-year old had been tried as an adult and served 13 years. (how do they charge a minor as an adult, anyway?) The 4 other juveniles served 6-7 years. I would have put a full-page ad in the newspaper to "END RACIAL PROFILING." Then I would take out a double full-page ad to say, "CONGRATULATIONS NYPD – YOU LET THE REAL CRIMINAL GET AWAY TO KILL AGAIN." Maybe the cops, district attorney, and judge should go serve a nice long time in prison and see how they like it.

The unabashed President still says they confessed; they were guilty. He concocted the brilliant preconceived analysis, "These young men do not exactly have the past of angels." What a scholarly legal mind he has. A lot of ignorant cops think the same way.

Drug abuse is a crime that warrants treatment. By the way, know this: All drug users are drug sellers. All of them dealers. If one drug user splits the cost of drugs with another, it's dealing. They do it constantly. If one of them happens to be a narc and entraps the other, they're caught for dealing. If someone gets caught with drugs, they can get out of trouble by making a deal with the police to make a 'drug buy' from their source, or friend or anybody. "Hello friend, can you get me some drugs?" "I guess so, friend." This sickening little game goes on in every police station from coast to coast, every day of the week. This is why our prisons are packed. People's lives are ruined, not just by the drugs, but by the system.

Joe Biden is going to be a busy man. We need to get it together. We need to work together and solve our common problems. The young people know it intuitively. They almost pushed Bernie Sanders into the job. He was right there after the Nevada primary. He gave a great victory speech that night. If only it wasn't for a ginormous flock of beautiful Black church ladies with very funny wide brim hats in South Carolina all lining up behind King-maker Jim Clyburn to deliver the state for Biden.

After that it was about whether or not the African American vote would be apathetic for the Democrat again like they had just exhibited in 2016, or would they line up to vote, 4 abreast as they did for Obama. It was about getting rid of the incumbent and everything else comes second. Why take a chance? Joe just isn't that exciting, but honestly, I think I've had enough excitement in the last 4 years. And I'll be so relieved to have a Democrat in the Oval Office, I want to take a 'wait and see' posture. He's not Bernie Sanders, but he's from the Clinton-Obama mold. He is very dependable, and I support him. He made a great speech the other day in which he warned Russia against interference in our elections. He would "impose substantial and lasting costs on state perpetrators," he cautioned. Those costs could include, "financial-sector sanctions, asset freezes, cyber response" and he really took nothing off the table to make his point. It was a tough message, and I like a President who makes it clear that he isn't going to put up with a foreign power messing with our rights. The opposite of what we have now.

He can solve the pandemic crisis. Covid-19 is not invincible, the first thing we need to do is fire up the World Health Organization again, full throttle. If there is anyone at WHO that needs to be replaced, the world needs to get that done, right away, but do it. The WHO is everywhere, like the coronavirus. We need the whole world to get on board to squash this thing. There is an average of over 250,000 new cases discovered every day worldwide. We can't have rogue states such as Sweden, Brazil, and the United States continue to deny scientific evidence and keep propagating disease with impunity.

Sweden wants to achieve 'Herd Immunity' and somehow claims that a 60% infection/immunity rate will stop the spread.

I've always thought the required percentage was closer to 85%, meaning 85% of the population carrying antibodies, and then even so, you always would want to vaccinate whenever possible. Sweden has already definitely experienced plenty of economic suffering, even though all their bars and restaurants are open, their citizens aren't all dumb enough to go hop on the coronavirus bandwagon. Business is way down. Tourism is a whole other question, no Stockholm this summer. And to date they've reached maybe 12% of their population and that's not even confirmed. It's an estimate. Out of a population of 10.1 million, they have 80,000 confirmed cases. That's less than 1% confirmed cases, 5700 dead so far. They have severely punished their senior citizens and other vulnerable groups. I truly hope they prove me wrong. I'm not one of those who's happy to see skyrocketing numbers in Florida, even though that bonehead Governor DeSantis, who his constituents now have nicknamed Governor DeSasterous still isn't mandating masks. But I'm also trying to make sense out of our response.

The human body makes antibodies, we can control this pandemic. Until there is a vaccine, we can control the spread of infection. We need social distancing guidelines. We need strict laws to make masks mandatory. Here in August, the Institute for Health Metrics and Evaluation (IHME) at the University of Washington is predicting that mandating masks would save at least 66,000 lives by December 1, 2020. That's right! In the United States, 228,271 total deaths would be projected with strict mandating of universal masks (95% usage) by December 1. However, projected partial easing of mandated mask requirements makes the number go up to a projected 295,010. I've been following this website, and IHME has been all over the place and had painted a much rosier picture back in April. I think they had better factor in for stupidity and double everything.

Although no one could have predicted the laxity in containing the virus we've witnessed across our country, which may have exacerbated the spread, I still can't understand what IHME means when they talk about "Mandates are re-imposed for 6 weeks if daily deaths reach 8 per million" Ok, so, in California, population 40 million we'd be talking about 320 deaths per day. It's never been that much, even on the worst day (213 deaths July 31). If I were Bill Gates and gave them $279 million in 2017, I'd want a little clarity, though.

Regardless, I can see the obvious value to masks, handwashing, disinfectants, social distancing (including quarantines), testing, and contact tracing. Nobody likes seatbelts either, but reflexively, we put them on. We're used to them (plus those annoying warning alarms). Masks are a little different because not only do they protect the wearer, but they also protect others. It's not surprising that the same people who don't care about the environment, are the same ones who don't care about making others sick or killing others with Covid-19.

If kids don't practice strict mandatory safety standards at school (testing, disinfectants, handwashing, masks, distancing, tracing, quarantine), not only will they get infected, with possible unknown long-term health issues, but another big factor is involved: They will spread infection through the schools to the whole community. Everyone knows, when school starts, the whole family gets sick. Kids from areas with high prevalence of disease, need to stay home. It's tough but there's no option.

Testing is a critical step in battling the pandemic. Why aren't we mass producing the necessary chemical reagents for wider distribution so we can get results in hours or days instead of weeks. County officials are complaining that they are forced to send test specimens to far away federal labs, sometimes out of state. They have the necessary equipment in their own facilities, but they lack the chemical reagents. It's 5 months since the first shortages and since the country started pleading for a federal response to the testing problems. The President and the Congress need to act.

I think a lot of tests are done on groups with certain symptoms, or high-risk groups in senior care facilities or prisons. I wonder why they don't test random group samples, for instance, a few thousand people in a given county. That would show the prevalence of the virus in an area. They talk about positivity rates, but I think most of those patients are getting tested because they feel they may have been exposed or have high risk jobs.

Speaking of testing, I would be interested to know how many people are positive for antibodies. There is a whole story that's been floating around, for quite a while now, that coronavirus antibodies don't necessarily protect you completely. Maybe that's another one of those baloney sandwiches like the one they were feeding us before about how masks don't protect you, you only wear them to protect other people. That was the line they were feeding us when there weren't enough masks to go around to cover all the hospital caregivers. Masks protect the person wearing them, too, don't ever let anyone tell you otherwise. Use your own brain to figure out that a mask can filter viruses out of the air, whether in droplets or aerosolized.

Those virus particles, thus filtered, don't end up in your nose and lungs.

Let's cut to the chase and talk about how our body's immune system fight's Covid-19. Viruses are genetic material plus a capsid to protect and aid in cell entry or exit. In the case of Covid-19, the genetic material is RNA, ribonucleic acid, a single-stranded molecule of genetic information, which requires a cell to help it to replicate.

Specific antibodies to the Covid-19 virus recognize the shape of that specific virus. They sort of snap on and bind to the virus and inhibit it from infecting cells where they would 'hide' and replicate. Another process is agglutination where more than one antibody-virus complex stick together, making it easier for our immune cells to target. A third beautiful way is for the antibody-virus complex to bind to an Fc receptor on a phagocytic cell triggering phagocytosis wherein the cell engulfs and destroys the complex. There is also a system of about 30 different proteins, produced in the liver, which travel in the blood plasma, called complement, which work in a cascade of reactions that work by identifying, coating, and leading to the destruction of viruses and other pathogens. In addition, cytotoxic T-cells recognize proteins (MHC) expressed on the surface of infected cells and release cytotoxic factors which kill the cell. Some viruses have adapted to prevent the expression of the MHC. Don't worry, we have natural killer (NK) cells which recognize if there are too way few MHC molecules. They sort of know something is wrong, so they kill those cells. These cytotoxic cells work in different ways, they punch holes in the membrane of the cell to allow killer enzymes called granzymes to enter the cell, or sometimes they just destroy the whole membrane. Another immune system protein, interferon, produced by infected cells themselves, can directly interfere with viral RNA replication. Interferon is also involved in cell signaling to protect other cells by increasing MHC expression in the neighboring cells.

You can spend 10 lifetimes studying cell signaling and you might figure out 10% of the most important reactions. In other words, there's a lot more to be learned. We can get a pretty good look at cells through electron microscopes, but the best microscopes can hardly visualize any of these molecular processes. It gets down to the atomic structure of the molecules. Molecular biology has evolved many techniques to study, identify and to modify these natural reactions.

The immune system can 'over-react' too severely and kill more cells than we would like, or cause other problems, producing an allergic reaction. Sometimes the lungs fill up with fluid, these fluids would be helpful in small quantities, but can be deadly if there is too much. Inflammation can help the body to heal, but acute inflammation can be harmful.

But antibodies are something you want to have, and you want to know it if you have them.

My friend from Brooklyn whose whole family tested positive for coronavirus antibodies, is going to a big wedding with 200 people this weekend. I would guess they'll be fine. I'd go if I had a positive antibody test. I like weddings. Maybe they just don't have enough Ab tests to go around. They'd probably only need about 5 billion or so. But don't think antibodies make you Superman. I'd still wear a mask.

There's been a lot of junk science, lately. Politicians and well-meaning journalists are briefing the public with false, inaccurate, or confusing statistics about 24 hours a day. As every medical statistician can tell you, there are three main types of lies: Lies, damn lies, and statistics.

Even the Lancet, a very highly respected peer-reviewed medical journal, had to print a retraction of a 'huge' hydroxychloroquine study. The study was so huge, it examined more cases than even existed at the time. A retraction means the results of a published study cannot be considered reliable. It can't be duplicated. This is inexcusable. The confusion it causes is intolerable. The drug was found to be associated with adverse events, but the whole study was retracted due to questions about the veracity of the underlying data. These adverse events have been common knowledge for decades. Just because a bad study is not reliable, it in no way proves that its conclusions are incorrect. But laypeople don't know what to make of it and conspiracy theories pop up all over like popcorn. Misinformation can be deadly.

As a side note, the Lancet took 12 years to retract a fake study which used bilgewater science to connect autism to the measles vaccine (MMR).

Here are just a few of the many questions that have yet to be definitively resolved by our scientific community:

1. Does immunity (antibody effectiveness) last. Are people getting re-infected, and if so what percentage (are the numbers statistically significant)? Where are the studies? The ones I've looked at are inconclusive, regarding antibody decay after a slight drop-off in the first 90 days.

2. Is the virus mutating. Some are theorizing that it is, but is that backed up by genome sequencing? What is the

extent of spread of any mutated strains? What I've found so far is that there might be mutations that are increasing the transmissibility. There may be enhanced replication meaning that it would spread easier. Another study says a spike protein may have developed on the capsid, that makes cell entry easier, so the strain competes with and replaces non-mutated strains, but without evidence that the strain causes a worse disease course. And nothing conclusive about whether the antibody is not still just as effective, or if vaccine development is going to be affected.

3. Some people have even speculated that the virus can only be contracted through airborne transmission, and not by contact with contaminated surfaces. This goes against everything I've ever known about sanitation, sterilization, and infection. Is there some proof behind these words?

It's been over 5 months since the first sparks of the coronavirus turned into a raging wildfire. It's time for some answers and some clear-cut directions. But instead the leaders of the free world are absent. The CDC has been told to stand down. Fifty states have been left to figure it out piecemeal, with little restriction to interstate travel. 195 countries all trying to solve the problem on their own, or to cobble together alliances and partnerships with each other. The WHO has saved the day in every corner of the globe. We'll figure this thing out one way or another, either we'll get it right the first time, or continue to pay the price as we dawdle along behind the Dawdler-in-Chief.

I can't see how it makes sense to draw policy around theories that antibodies won't protect us. Even if we hunker down and wait for a vaccine, immunity is all we can hope for. Yes, we can continue to wear masks, wash hands, increase testing, and stay socially distant. Yes, contact tracing and isolation works, if testing results are received in timely fashion. But let's assume the worst and see where it leads us: What if antibodies are degrading, and the virus is continuously mutating? Ok, we've been exposed, so, now our bodies have responded by repeatedly generating white blood cells that evolve into Memory B cells in a highly complex process within the lymph nodes and other germinal centers such as the spleen. They emerge as plasma cells producing large quantities of antibodies to the specific antigen they were exposed to. But in addition, our bodies also possess T cells, which attack and destroy all types of infected cells. Nobody can predict what different strains can evolve. There are no guarantees, everyone is different, but let's say it would be safe to predict that in general we could expect a milder course of the disease the second time around.

The alternative is to live out the rest of our lives forever with Grubhub deliveries and Zoom conferences.

So, we'll have to do everything we can to stay fit and in good health, and that's not going to hurt us even if all of the antibodies do remain viable. Quitting smoking and drinking, losing weight, exercising, those are not bad things.

The Lancet editor, Richard Horton, accused the American President of a "crime against humanity" for defunding the WHO. I couldn't have put it any better, except I would say also that the people who voted for him committed a 'crime against humanity' in the voting booths, too. Horton has accused British

Prime Minister Boris Johnson of misconduct for telling his people that they were well prepared even though their stockpile of personal protective equipment had been inadequate even for years before the crisis. Horton went on to continue his blistering exposé of the abandonment of standard scientific advice, which called for testing, tracing, and isolation. As a result, the UK suffered horrendous infection and death: 46,000 deaths out of 306,000 confirmed cases. Of course, the U.S. has also endured horrible consequences: 155,000 deaths out of 4,600,000 cases. Britain is still seeing 800 new cases a day these days while we're looking at over 60,000 a day. While the world cries out for leadership through the pandemic, both leaders have decided to adopt the 'go it alone' strategy, generating millions of infected citizens to instead amplify the worldwide spread.

Another friend of mine is in the hospital as I write this. She called me from the hospital after vanishing for 5 days. She sounded so weak and miserable, the exact opposite of the person I knew. She told me she had the virus and couldn't hold anything down. She was having difficulty breathing. Everything hurt until her temperature came down from over 102. They wouldn't let her out of bed. They couldn't give her anything to eat, and she was being given Zofran which controls nausea, she didn't know what other medications she was getting. When she needed to take a Tylenol, they only allowed her one sip of water. She begged me to stay in touch and gave my name to the staff so I could discuss her condition with them. She cried "I don't want to just vanish off the face of the earth." I consoled her, telling her that it was a very good sign that her temperature had come down, and I reminded her that she was in probably the best hospital in Orange County. She wasn't allowed any visitors.

When I called back in two days, she sounded a little better and said that her test results had come back negative for coronavirus. She had eaten a little bit of scrambled eggs. She was drinking plenty of water, walking around some, and feeling a little better. I was so happy, I forgot how infuriated I was that it had taken 7 days to get the negative test results back.

Now comes the third act of this little drama. It has yet to be written. Will she be ok? She's been in an area of the hospital reserved for probable Covid patients for 7 days and has at least a couple more days to go. I doubt they will move her to another part of the hospital now. She still has to recover from whatever bug she actually is suffering from and get the hell out of there without contracting a nosocomial (hospital acquired) Covid-19 infection. When they release her will she be an asymptomatic carrier? Is her mom is going to be ok, she'll need to quarantine for sure, at least I would.

How many times do you think the people caring for her changed their gowns, masks and gloves, etc.? As they buzzed about like mosquito vectors from patient to patient, throughout the whole ward full of virus patients, you would think each caregiver would need dozens of changes per day. You know that wasn't happening. Maybe she had a dedicated nurse staying in her room, I hope so.

The other thing to keep worrying about is a possible false negative test. I would think they will repeat the Covid-19 test as well as an Antibody test, but who knows.

Remdesivir is a broad-spectrum antiviral medication that has shown promise in shortening the recovery period for Covid-19. The National Institute of Health (NIH) has approved its use for hospitalized patients with poor blood oxygen saturation levels (at or below SpO2 94), those requiring supplemental oxygen, as well as patients who are on a ventilator. While many studies are more or less going on under chaotic conditions in the most critical settings, with many patients in their last desperate throws of life, the promising results are being painstakingly tabulated and reviewed for safety and efficacy. As I write this, its mortality benefit has yet to be conclusively shown. Future trials, however, will most likely demonstrate its usefulness, given the other desirable benefits.

According to the WHO, dexamethasone, a well-known corticosteroid anti-inflammatory and immunosuppressant has been shown to reduce 28-day mortality in 30% of patients on ventilators and 20% of those requiring only oxygen. This was demonstrated by over 2104 patents randomly allocated to take dexamethasone, compared to 4321 patients concurrently allocated to usual care in the UK national clinical trial, aptly named RECOVERY. The treatment is safe for children and the elderly, but pregnant women were given oral prednisolone, a milder corticosteroid or hydrocortisone injection. Thank you, University of Oxford for looking at this generic drug that no pharmaceutical company would ever waste one dollar looking at since they can't rob everybody without a 20-year patent on some new 'Wonder Drug'.

Human blood is composed of red cells, white cells, platelets, and about 55% of it is the liquid portion called plasma. Plasma contains water, salts (electrolytes), and proteins. One type of proteins in the plasma are antibodies. Blood from patients who have recovered from Covid-19 contains antibodies which are specific for the Covid-19 virus. Treatment with convalescent plasma is an investigational therapy reserved for seriously ill patients. Major risks include allergic reactions, lung damage and difficulty breathing, and transmission of infections such as HIV or hepatitis B and C.

Great promise has been shown by antiviral monoclonal antibodies in current trials. A simplistic way to think of these drugs is that Memory B cells are cloned, and they produce antibodies which attack the virus. Some of the techniques used in the manufacturing of this category of pharmaceuticals involve some of the most complicated microbiological processes you could ever imagine. Treatments and cures for multiple sclerosis, rheumatoid arthritis, psoriasis, cancer, asthma, Crohn's disease, and a whole list of other devastating diseases have benefited from this brilliant medical technology. Maybe we can add one more to the list.

Various blood thinners have been successfully employed to save lives by preventing Covid-19 related blood clots that can result in thrombotic occlusions of small to medium peripheral pulmonary arteries (in the lung). Higher dosages may be effective to control these. Blood clots are known to cause heart attacks, strokes, and deadly pulmonary embolisms as well as many other complications.

Humidifiers have been a relief to many patients, even including some of the less serious cases. And they have even produced superior results compared to heat moisture exchangers, by increasing humidification.

Dextromethorphan, a common cough suppressant, and Guaifenesin, a mucus expectorant, are well tolerated by hospitalized patients as well as those at home. So are acetaminophen, ibuprofen and naproxen sodium for fever and pain.

Turning some of the sickest patients onto their stomachs, reffered to as prone positioning, has often shown immediate improvement in blood oxygen saturation. Patients who are ventilated are sometimes turned over for 16 hours a day. This improves oxygenation to many parts of the lung by relieving pressure from the weight of the body. Studies are examining the intuitive logical extension of trying "proning" on patients who simply need supplemental oxygen by nasal canula. This positioning has often been used to help avoid decubitus ulcers (bedsores), which need to be avoided, especially in ICU patients and others hospitalized for extended periods of time.

Mechanical ventilators have become more and more effective in increasing survival with the knowledge that's been gathered about such subjects as preventing blood clotting and fine-tuning the body's immune system response. Originally it was feared that patients requiring ventilation had little chance of survival. Some New York hospitals were saying they were experiencing 88% mortality rates. That might be due to the makeshift ICU's, abnormally high rates of comorbidity with diseases like diabetes for example in the Bronx, and a severe lack of ability to count correctly. What else is new? After all, they're doctors, not mathematicians, maybe their i-phones needed charging (they're so lost without them). With all the chaos and hospitals bursting at the seams, patients who had recovered and had been sent home, after being taken off the ventilators, were being counted among the dead. Also, patients who were still alive who were still intubated and fighting the disease, were being included in the tally as dead. More recent studies at Emory University and Vanderbilt University are figuring mortality at 30% and under. It's a complicated topic, but it would be nice if, as treatments and outcomes approve overall, we would see 80% and higher survival post ventilation. Unfortunately, many of these that recover will be left with irreversible lung scarring that can affect their quality of life. Regaining lung function can be a lengthy process and it can remain diminished to varying degrees. Other big residual problems include PTSD and severe depression.

Increased oxygen or nitric oxide, a breathing dilator, can be tried first. Patients must maintain arterial oxygen saturation greater than 90%. Ventilators are not used until a patient is in severe respiratory distress, without any options. One doctor said, "They're dying on the ventilator, not necessarily dying because of being on a ventilator." The machine gives you a chance to recover. But, as it breathes for you, your diaphragm and other muscles involved in breathing can become weak. Acute lung injury is also a possible danger that can result usually due to overinflating the lungs.

Some patients tolerate intubation better than others. Most require sedation and analgesics as well as other medications. Propofol (or as doctors call it, Milk of Amnesia) and midazolam are commonly used for sedation, along with very strong pain drugs, such as morphine or fentynl. Paralytics like succinylcholine or vecuronium help to prevent throat spasms.

Some current estimates are that around 5% of hospitalized Covod-19 patients do not survive. It's goes up to almost 20% if there are other serious underlying health conditions.

Hundreds and thousands of Doctors and other researchers are in this fight, and because of them, I truly believe we will win. Not by magical thinkers like the President and his obnoxious campaign team.

Not enough can be said about our brave hospital workers, who literally step into the warzone up to seven days a week, to put their lives on the line to save these patients. Nurses, doctors, respiratory therapists, radiologic technicians, lab workers, clerks, housekeepers, food service staff, pharmacy staff, environmental staff, medical students and countless others make it all work.

It's hard to hear these fearless workers begging for help and getting no federal response whatsoever. Some even have to continue without a state response, or their county or their city; they're the ones making hospital gowns out of trash bags. I saw one who was forced to make a face mask out of a plastic top of a salad to-go container. It's so painful listening to that dunce Pence claim, "All the hospitals have everything they need." It's appalling. Are masks supposed to be worn from one patient to the next? For the whole shift? All kinds of reports are out there where people say they were told to reuse their masks. That's in the hospitals. Now, what about the mandates to wear a mask in public? How many days can someone wear the same mask? Let's be honest, people could change their masks more often. This is where the CDC should be giving clear guidance.

For decades, scientists have considered the National Institute of Health (NIH) to be the very pinnacle of humanity. So far, it still shows the world how American leadership in medicine can benefit mankind. Normally, they gallantly tackle the job of coordinating all types of research all over the country and proudly share knowledge with the whole world. These days the White House has been passing out the research grants for vaccine research, etc. That's a big mistake, but here we go again.

A lot of people don't realize that doctors from all over the world refer cases to NIH when they can't make the diagnosis.

They are like a bulldog that will never let go. No disease is too rare; they don't give up. Doctors at NIH solve every medical problem no matter how long it may take, even if it takes years. The main hospital in Bethesda, Maryland has patient rooms on one side of the tower and research labs on the other. The huge campus is very modern and quite amazing.

They consistently stand up to phony schemes, charlatans, quacks and politicians who would take us back to the Dark Ages when the earth was flat, diseases were caused by sin, and bloodletting was the cure of the day. NIH has sometimes been accused of wavering in the face of political pressures but remains the top scientific agency in the world. So, don't worry, rest easy America, NIH won't let you down.

Compare them to the CDC, which has folded like a cheap suit leaving the country to wallow in disease and death. Hello! Nobody home. They couldn't be counted on to pass out tissues, let alone to make sure hospitals have the personnel and equipment they need. What about senior care facilities, food supply and restaurants, schools, prisons, public transportation, other essential workers for starters? They really dropped the ball. There are tons of great people at CDC, they've been stripped of their power.

They've been relegated to a façade of what they once were.

The Secretary of Health and Human Services and sycophant Alex Azar, tasked with carrying out the federal response to the pandemic, has a very easy job. He just has to make sure that nothing ever gets done. So, he brilliantly ordered hospitals to send Covid-19 data directly to the White House and not to send the data to CDC anymore. Another agency bites the dust. Just in case there were any scientists left with any control at CDC, gotta get them out of the way before they make any trouble. The data on deaths, hospital admissions, staff shortages, ICU beds, Personal Protective Equipment, ventilators and who knows what else will now become available on a need to know basis, only. In other words, nobody needs to know, so it won't be available. The experts are worried. The experienced data collectors at CDC can go do something else. But be sure the White House will give us the data they want us to have. And they would never lie to us, right? We trust the President, right? Let's hope the New York Times is already gearing up to collect this additional data that the world will need.

The Pharmacist-in-Chief heard a rumor from the people he calls "the best people in the world," (right-wing radio hosts?) that the anti-malarial drug, hydroxychloroquine was in high demand all over the world to treat coronavirus. He would score big on what he referred to as the "game changer." He called India's Prime minister Modi to beg him to let him get his hands on a big shipment. "You know they put a stop to it because they wanted it for India," he told Sean Hannity. Ha! What a pigeon. They were so happy to dump that cheap drug that would soon become as obsolete to treat Covid-19 as yesterday's newspaper. The Prime Minister was "great," he said, and he had managed to talk them out of 29 million doses, he later claimed. Reuters reported it to be 50 million tablets. A total of 66 million doses were by all accounts abandoned in the federal stockpile when the FDA pulled its emergency use authorization. The minor benefits are dwarfed by the deadly risks. Peter Navarro had been hawking this hoard of pills all over the place and had to cancel the whole distribution. He's still jabbering his nonsense.

The main drawback here is that this drug knocks your electrocardiogram (ECG) out of whack. It causes a significant risk of QTc interval prolongation. The Q-T interval refers to the time for the heart's ventricular depolarization and repolarization. It normally takes generally from 400 – 440 milliseconds (ms). The QTc interval is considered prolonged if it is over 450 ms in men and 470 ms in women. In one study it was shown hydroxychloroquine causes development of prolongation of the QTc interval of up to a total of 500 ms in 19% of patients, and over 7% of patients had a developed a change of over 60 ms over baseline. It's like a heart hiccup that you don't want. Not if you don't want to develop a deadly rhythm called Torsades de Pointes or fatal polymorphic ventricular tachycardia or ventricular fibrillation. The chambers of the heart flutter uselessly, not filling up and pumping out blood resulting in low blood pressure, loss of consciousness or death. So keep your defibrillators handy.

You have to wonder why Breitbart is pushing hydroxychloroquine and going so far as posting this medical disinformation on Facebook, Twitter and YouTube. The video, which was later banned by the three social media giants, says, "the virus has a cure, it's called hydroxychloroquine, zinc, and Zithromax. You don't need masks." The President picked it up from Breitbart and re-tweeted it.

The video featured people in white coats on the steps of the Supreme Court, mostly doctors, who didn't seem to understand or even believe that 150,000 Americans have died so far from this virus. The star of the show was Stella Immanuel, the Looney Tune from Cameroon. She's a pediatrician/minister who works in an office in a strip mall in Houston. Her group Fire Power Ministry mixes wacked out medical theories with revelations about 'sex dreams' with demons and spirits. She is a complete embarrassment to all her fellow graduates of the medical school of the University of Calabar in Nigeria. She is a certified basket case that has claimed that aliens and reptilians run the government. Do you want to take medical advice from a doctor who lectures that illuminati and witches are trying to destroy the world through gay marriage and children's toys like Harry Potter, Pokémon, and Hannah Montana? How about she's claimed that endometriosis is caused by women having sex with witches and demons in their dreams (endometriosis is tissue similar to that which normally lines the uterus growing outside of the uterus, typically caused by retrograde menstruation or hormonal problems). In 2015 she claimed that vaccines are being developed to stop people from being religious. Her sermons have proven that this might actually not be such a terrible idea, if only it were true. The President "thought she was very impressive." She's a real slap in the face to the Texas Medical Board. Is this real, or just another news-cycle distraction.

The University of Oxford in England did a study on over 11,000 Covid-19 patients to examine hydroxychloroquine, and several other treatments. The hydroxychloroquine portion of the study randomly split patients into two groups. They gave the drug to one of the groups, which consisted of 1,542 patients. The sample size, meaning the number of patients receiving the drug, and the control group are determined by computing the number of patients necessary to achieve a statistically significant result. When they compared the results of the hydroxychloroquine patients to the rest, who received the usual care, they found that 25.7% of the patients treated with hydroxychloroquine had died after 28 days. In the other group, the 28-day mortality rate was only 23.5%. Officially announcing, "This is not a cure for Covid," the trial study stopped using the drug. In the study, called a double-blind clinical trial, neither the patient, nor the healthcare professionals knew who was in which group. All patients understand and agree to assume the risks. They sign up to potentially benefit themselves and mankind. This scientifically designed study showed increased mortality of 2.2% in the treatment group. That means that 1,542 x .022 = 34 people gave their lives to prove that we can forget about hydroxychloroquine to treat Covid-19. Thirty-four human beings died because they made the sacrifice to participate in the study. Can we please not forget these brave volunteers? We already know our dumbass President doesn't like losers; he only likes winners. Actually, I don't think he understands any of this, but I don't like him because his words cause pain, suffering and death. He's dangerous, as we have been admonished about so many times before. We were warned that he'd ruin the country.

Concomitant administration of the antibiotic azithromycin (Zithromax), as the White House (and Stella!!) recommended, causes an even greater percentage of patients to suffer these side effects. Zithromax also destroys a lot of healthy bacteria leading to increased chances of developing dangerous Clostridium difficile (C-diff) infections which can result in pseudomembranous colitis or toxic megacolon, perforation of the colon, sepsis or peritonitis. Thank you Mr. President and your gaggle of quacks in white coats.

This debate about aerosol transmission versus droplet transmission versus infection through contact with contaminated surfaces is very fascinating and helpful for air conditioner protocols, but not for the average person. We need to wear masks, quit touching our faces so much, use disinfectant wipes, and maintain 6 feet separation. The moron President wants to berate Dr. Fauci for first telling people not to wear masks, and now telling them to wear them. What a classic idiot. There weren't enough masks. Doctors, nurses, ambulance drivers, didn't have masks, so they didn't want the public to compete for supplies, and Dr. Fauci explained that. This is 5 months later. Free masks should be everywhere all over the world by now, no more excuses.

We are right on the edge technologically to be able to easily monitor spread and institute contact tracing world-wide. Michael Bloomberg and Johns Hopkins have built a leading contact tracing organization, and have no doubt helped the New York/New Jersey/Connecticut region cool things down to a level they could cope with. It's estimated that the United States needs a 100,000-person force to accomplish this task. You still would have a lot of stupidity (it's the USA after all), but something is better than nothing. We need to commandeer the necessary resources whether it's through the Defense Procurement Act and/or some International Agreement, we can shut this thing down. Can Facebook and Google and Apple help us here or are they only capable of spying on all of us for corporate financial gain. The government needs to step in and force them to get it done. The manufacturers of the world need to get the huge number of necessary masks, gloves, disinfectant wipes, sanitizers, etc., made. It won't be done unless the governments of the world work benevolently for the good of all humanity in a concerted effort. C'mon you jerk, you want to Make America Great Again by bringing back nationwide slavery, this is your chance to boss everybody around (boss lots of companies around) and force them to produce and to do something they otherwise do not want to do. The profit margins are not going to motivate an effective response. As an example, the reason you can't find toilet paper at your store is not because of hording. It's because people are staying home, and not using public restrooms at work, schools, stores, etc. The distribution of commercial type cases of toilet paper has been decimated, but rapid repackaging and redistribution wouldn't be economically feasible. We're left with a slow, calculated, ramp up to maximize profits.

Scenes of crops being plowed under that were destined for restaurants across the country are abhorrent in the current predicament of long lines for emergency food pantries and giant food bank operations even requiring the services of the National Guard in some states. But without the government to step in and start distributing food, milk, and other crops, it goes to waste, while kids go hungry. Good show.

It doesn't stop at food; all durable goods need to have dependable markets. Even medical supply chains can break down, too. Trucking, retail, manufacturing, they are all critical links, and they deserve the attention of the federal government. Why isn't the military giving us a hand? Hundreds of thousands of troops could definitely be put to good use, during a state of emergency.

Capitalism will not be the answer here. Why invest money if you're uncertain of the profit. It's incredibly expensive to tool up quickly, to set up distribution, establish supply chains, and to employ and train people. The motivation here has to be the benefit to the end user, and unfortunately, the connection between supply and demand, as a driver of production, is based firmly on the benefit to the manufacturers and their shareholders. Investors like a sure thing. Lose your money, and you're done. Sit on the sidelines and you're ok. Make one big mistake and blow your whole career. Being smart in business means playing it safe. We need the federal government, indeed all the governments of the world, to step in and get us to where we need to be.

The equitable distribution of supplies of Personal Protective Equipment needs to be an international priority. The equitable distribution of medicine and disinfectant supplies needs to be an international priority. Public cooperation needs to be an international priority. We need sturdy leaders who inspire trust and compliance with all scientific mandates.

Instead, we see not wearing a mask as the new right-wing political fashion statement. You don't need a red (ugly) MAGA hat, you just have to march around town defiantly with no mask. To get 10 extra wacko points, you can scoff at everyone who does wear a mask or does something exhibiting social distancing, or social consciousness of any kind.

We can't be satisfied with a lying buffoon who can't think of anything besides re-election, and personal gain. And the bonus is he gives us 'smaller' government and a world full of hate and not much else. We need our government to be stronger than ever. Thousands of people working alone can't build a bridge, but working together, we can do anything. But we need leaders who lift our hearts, raise our spirits, and encourage technology and science to help make our lives easier.

President Biden will be such a welcome hero. We can bang the CDC back together. We can reassemble the Environmental Protection Agency. We can have justice reform. We can revamp banking regulations and the tax codes. We can reign in banks, insurance companies, pharmaceutical companies and Amazon, too. We can pick up the pieces and start over.

About the Author

The writer, Charlie Pearlman is one of the few Baby Boomers living in Southern California, who was actuality born there. Maybe he never had the good sense to get out. He's a father of 4, living in Newport Beach, California. A life-long student and entrepreneur, he's currently working in the Financial Industry. He considers himself to be a very lucky person. He enjoys spending time with his wife (pretty good, huh?), traveling (before), going to restaurants (before) and enjoying the ocean breeze together. He's known to spend time working out, running, playing chess, studying political issues and surfing the internet as well as communicating with family and friends. He's never missed a chance to vote, and more specifically to vote for the Democrat every single time.

Although his dad was a Merchant Marine and served in the South Pacific during WWII, his mother certainly never raised him to be a soldier. He was lucky to avoid the Vietnam draft when the Draft Lottery missed him by 3 days, while around that time a lot of his radical political persuasions were developing during his college years at UC Berkeley. His highest military achievement was in the Cub Scouts where he proudly earned a Wolf patch for camping. He's very concerned about environmental issues, and a true believer in science and research, two very important subjects for the survival and betterment of mankind.

UC Berkeley Chemistry/Physics
Southwestern University School of Law
American University of Antigua College of Medicine

CPSIA information can be obtained
at www.ICGtesting.com
Printed in the USA
LVHW080027290920
667368LV00010B/183/J